Paths to GOD

Paths to GOD

Building a Christian Life in the 21st Century

Bishop Javier Echevarria

 Scepter

This edition published in April 2010 by
Scepter Publishers
PO Box 211
New York, NY 10018 USA

Text Design: Rose Design

Printed in the United States of America

ISBN-13: 978-1-59417-085-0

Contents

Author's Preface to the English Edition

Almost ten years ago, in desiring to contribute to the spiritual renewal underway during the Jubilee Year 2000, I wrote a few considerations about the being and the task of a Christian. At that time I sensed what every ordained minister—both priests and bishops—feels: the urgent necessity to dedicate himself, both in his preaching and in his dealings with souls, to this life according to the Spirit (cf. Rom 8:9), in which all of us as Christians must participate.

These reflections offer a guide to following Jesus Christ through the paths of the spiritual life. Especially in the case of lay Christians, to whom I direct myself in a special way, these paths follow the circumstances that their secular condition places before them: their family life, work, friendships, and suffering.

A holy priest of our age, St. Josemaría Escrivá, taught that "the Christian is obliged to become *alter Christus, ipse Christus*, another Christ, Christ himself." In virtue of baptism, we all are made as priests of our own existence, "to offer spiritual sacrifices acceptable to God through Jesus Christ" (1 Peter 2:5), and to carry out each of our actions in a spirit of obedience to the will of God, continuing in this way the mission of God-made-man" (*Christ Is Passing By*, 96). This is why the priesthood of ordained ministers and of the faithful, while being essentially distinct, are mutually related to each other. We cooperate in realizing the only mission of the Church, which is to bring the salvation of Christ to all the corners of the earth.

I am particularly happy that the English translation of this book arrives during the Year for Priests that His Holiness Benedict XVI proclaimed on occasion of the 150th anniversary of the *dies natalis* of the holy Curé of Ars. The Pope wishes us to recognize more fully the immense gift to the Church that the Lord has given in the priesthood, and with confidence to implore the Divine Goodness for many holy priests throughout the world. These ministers of Christ normally come from Christian families, where education in the faith constitutes an essential part of the mission entrusted to parents.

Seen in this way, it is clear that this Year affects us all—clergy and laity, each according to the vocation and the mission received within the Mystical Body of Christ. During these months, and always, I hope that all of us might strive to become more like Christ, and to make him present in the crossroads of this world.

Ten years ago I wrote that, "every Christian journey takes place within the Church and, frequently, is guided by the help of spiritual masters." Like thousands of others, I had the privilege of an exceptional guide, St. Josemaría. The many years that I passed at the side of this holy pastor of souls, the assiduous meditation of his writings and of his counsels, and his example, have profoundly marked my soul. For this reason it is only logical that these pages should be frequently interwoven with his words. In doing this I am not merely moved by gratitude, but rather by the fact that his teaching contains clear lights and decisive impetus for bettering our Christian living, now and forever.

Rome, November 6, 2009

PART I

Sources of Christian Life

God:
Father of Infinite Mercy

S ons and daughters of God. That is what we are, as the Gospel proclaims, although many people still don't realize it. God's call to be his children in Christ, divine filiation, is a treasure much richer than any on earth. If people were truly aware of this reality, our world would be a very different place, without hatred or discrimination, without backbiting or slander, a world where the simple and clear truth reigned. There would be no room for abuse or manipulation, and solidarity would grow, since the realization that we are God's children fosters true fraternity.

John Paul II wanted us to prepare for the great Jubilee along a Trinitarian pathway, a path both of spiritual life and of study and intellectual work. He asked us to go to the Father (1999) in the Son (1997) through the Holy Spirit (1998), and then in the year 2000 to *give glory to the Trinity, from whom everything in the world and in history comes and to whom everything returns*" (*Tertio Millennio Adveniente*, no. 55). This preparation recalls the first years of his pontificate, when John Paul II offered us a magnificent trilogy of encyclicals dedicated to each of the divine Persons. *Redemptor Hominis* and *Dominum et Vivificantem*, spoke of the Son and the Holy Spirit, while *Dives in Misericordia* led us to the Father, "rich in mercy," with a profound commentary on the parable of the prodigal son.

We see today a widespread crisis in human fatherhood that makes it hard for many to view God as Father. Certainly this problem is not new. Christ himself, in his efforts to teach the people of his time to trust in God and pray to him as Father, had to combat a stereotype of the Creator as a remote and distant Being. But still we might ask: Isn't our present difficulty in discovering God as Father due also to modern cultural factors?

Many young people today lack an authentic image of a father (and sometimes of a mother) to help them grasp the truth that they are God's daughters or sons. A broken family deprives children of affection and security that only comes from the indissoluble union of a father and a mother. It's also true that many parents, for various reasons, neglect the importance of their own paternity or maternity.

On a more theoretical plane, variations of feminist theology object that God's masculine name lends legitimacy to unjust patriarchal social structures. John Paul II confronted this objection in his encyclical *Mulieris Dignitatem*, showing that God's fatherhood has a fully divine and spiritual meaning, one that transcends any bodily dimensions. God loves us with an infinite heart, both paternal and maternal at the same time.

In contemporary culture as well, confidence in reason and science is undergoing a crisis while other values are held in high esteem such as the dignity of the person, the role of women, a hunger for peace, respect for volunteer initiatives and social work. There is also a real longing for family, since every human being, like it or not, is a son or daughter in his or hers deepest recesses. We can also see a religious reawakening, a clear sign of the need for God, although this spiritual resurgence is mixed with great ignorance or an indifference linked to a breakdown in the very notion of truth.

Discovering God's Fatherly Affection

John Paul II constantly exhorted us to not be afraid, to foster the virtue of hope, to overcome the devil's original temptation to distrust God, which led to the fall of our first parents. Today, too, the devil promotes suspicion and mistrust of God, despite his being *clementissime Pater*, a most merciful Father, as the Eucharistic prayer calls him. The world has great need of that fatherhood to find peace and true happiness.

By divine providence, beginning in 1948 I lived alongside St. Josemaría Escrivá. His life and words always witnessed to what was the central reality for him: the conviction that God is a Father. He had a vivid memory of October 16, 1931, the day God granted him the experience of a prayer that he described as among the most elevated of his life. "I felt God acting within me. He was making spring forth in my heart and on my lips, with the force of something imperatively necessary, the tender invocation: 'Abba! Pater!' I was out on the street, in a streetcar. . . . Probably I made that prayer out loud. And I walked the streets of Madrid for maybe an hour, maybe two, I can't say. Time passed without my being aware of it. People must have thought I was crazy. I was contemplating, with lights that were not mine, that amazing truth. It was like a lighted coal burning in my soul, never to be extinguished."[1]

God is a Father. He gives us life, and watches over us with infinite affection. His providential care never leaves us. Sometimes, certainly, it can be hard to discern the paths of his providence or comprehend his ways, but we can always abandon ourselves trustingly in his fatherly arms.

Seen in this light, life takes on its true and deep meaning and overflows with supernatural and human richness. Trivial concerns, monotony, daily duties thought to be valueless routines, all this disappears. Family life, work, and daily occupations are seen as a divine gift and gladly accepted as a way of serving. There is no room for a cold, narrow attitude, half pharisaical and half puritanical, that reduces religion to an effort to satisfy a demanding God by obeying rules. Nor is there

---

1. Andrés Vázquez de Prada, *The Founder of Opus Dei*, vol. 1. New York, NY: Scepter, 2001, 334.

room for superficiality or routine in the relationship with God. Someone convinced he is a child of God and aware of God's constant and caring nearness, finds incomprehensible this view of religion. One's life is harmoniously interwoven with the loving providence of our Father God; for no human being in this world is ever alone and God is always at his children's side.

It is true that painful situations will sometimes arise that our limited human understanding finds it hard to comprehend. But even then we can never doubt God's love. With the security that faith brings, we have to look at Jesus. God sent his Son into the world so that we too could be *sons in the Son* and, looking at him, would realize how immense his love is. The Father manifests his fatherhood through the words and life of his Eternal Son, who entered human history when he took on our nature. Christ, by his deeds and words, reveals the Father to us and shows us his infinite love.

The Gospel of St. John records an unusual request by the apostle Philip at the Last Supper: "Lord, show us the Father, and we shall be satisfied." Jesus replied forcefully: "Have I been with you so long, and yet you do not know me, Philip? He who has seen me has seen the Father."[2] This moved the apostles to exclaim: "Now you are speaking plainly, not in any figure! Now we know that you know all things, and need none to question you; by this we believe that you came from God."[3]

The Father remains invisible, but his voice can be heard at certain points in the Gospel narrative. At Jesus' Baptism, he gives testimony to the mission of the Word made man: "Thou art my beloved Son; with thee I am well pleased."[4] At the Transfiguration, he speaks similar words: "This is my beloved Son; listen to him."[5] On both occasions, the Father points out the path that leads to him: Listen to Christ, follow him, contemplate him.

---

2. Jn 14:8–9.
3. Jn 16:29–30.
4. Mk 1:11.
5. Mk 9:7.

Jesus in turn speaks continually of the Father, of his love, his goodness and mercy, his fatherly care for all mankind; he teaches us the prayer *par excellence*, the *Our Father*. He reveals the Father by his words and his life. Working miracles, forgiving sins, being moved and even weeping, he shows us both God's omnipotence and his mercy. He does this in the great events of his public life and also (and I wish to stress this, because it is not always given the importance it deserves) through the events of his ordinary life, the thirty years he spent living and working in Nazareth to help support his family. Jesus wishes to show us that we are to act as the Father's children in daily life.

The end of Jesus' life on earth brought the event that fully revealed God's fatherly mercy: the Cross. The Father's love for us went to the extreme of asking his Son to make the supreme sacrifice of his life for our sakes. And Jesus, the Word incarnate, gave himself so that through his death, lovingly accepted, we might be redeemed from sin, experience God's love, and so be able to love our heavenly Father.

As the fruit of the Cross, the Father and Son sent the Holy Spirit to incorporate us into Christ through the power of grace and grant us the gift of divine filiation. "You have received," writes St. Paul to the Romans, "the spirit of sonship. When we cry, 'Abba! Father!' it is the Spirit himself bearing witness with our spirit that we are children of God."[6] The Holy Spirit's powerful manifestation on the day of Pentecost was to give the apostles the strength they needed to bear witness, with the freedom and daring of children, that Jesus is the Only-Begotten sent by the Father.

The Son and the Spirit visibly manifested themselves two thousand years ago, and they continue their action, in a manner invisible but real, until the end of time. We are sons and daughters of the Father in the incarnate Son, through the Holy Spirit. A Christian's identity consists in being a child of God in Christ and therefore—words of St. Josemaría that I often heard—knowing himself to be *alter Christus*,

---

6. Rom 8:15–16.

ipse Christus, another Christ, Christ himself: in being "Christ who is passing by" in the midst of mankind.

Living as Daughters and Sons of God

The sending of the Son and the Paraclete and their efficacious presence among us enable us to share in the love of the Three Divine Persons. Then what we do in ordinary life no longer is done as servants but as God's friends, as his children, with a filial freedom expressed in love. And when through frailty we fail in generosity and distance ourselves from God like the prodigal son in the parable, we know that recourse to the Sacrament of Penance can restore the grace flowing from Christ's redeeming Blood poured out for us on the Cross. Repenting in this sacrament, as the prodigal son did, we are lovingly embraced by the Father who cures us of our selfishness and restores to us the freedom of love. We once again take up our work and daily activities as God's children.

But like Christ we attain the freedom of true children by embracing his Cross. In a prayer on April 28, 1963, the Founder of Opus Dei expressed this with deep personal conviction: "You, Lord, have helped me understand that to have the Cross means finding happiness and joy. And the reason, which I now see more clearly than ever, is this: having the Cross means being identified with Christ, means being Christ, and therefore a son of God."[7]

God's fatherhood accompanies us at every moment. It reveals the holy meaning of suffering and death, taking away, as St. Paul said, their "sting." God doesn't free us from suffering, but he removes the sadness and bitterness, while asking us to alleviate the sufferings of others and forget our own, as our Mother Mary did at the foot of the Cross. We must walk daily along this path, with the deep conviction that we are daughters and sons of God. Thus we will always be, as St. Josemaría Escrivá wished, "sowers of peace and of joy."

---

7. Cf. Letter from the Prelate, September 1, 2001.

Knowing Jesus Christ and Making Him Known

Under the action of the Holy Spirit, the Christian vocation, a gift and call from the Father, impels us to configure ourselves to Jesus Christ. Clothed in Christ in the Sacrament of Baptism and strengthened in the Eucharist with communion in his Body and Blood, we are made sharers in his filial condition and mission. We have been sent by Christ—as he was sent by his Father—to proclaim, by our life and deeds, the Good News of the Kingdom of God.

"The time is fulfilled, and the kingdom of God is at hand; repent, and believe in the gospel."[1] With these words Christ began his mission. With Christ and in Christ, through our actions and words, by the grace of Baptism we can proclaim to those around us: Believe in the Gospel! Open your minds and hearts to Christ; trust in the Savior!

Traveling the roads of Palestine and announcing the coming of his Father's kingdom, Jesus and his followers one day arrived at the region of Caesarea Philippi, a place of religious and cultural contrasts not far from pagan territory. There he asked his disciples: "Who do men

---

1. Mk 1:15.

say that the Son of Man is?"[2] As St. John says in his Gospel, the Master needed no one to tell him what was in somebody's heart. He knew perfectly well what effect his teaching had in the souls of his listeners. Some showed themselves more open to faith and conversion; others were not yet well disposed to accepting God's grace. Already, too, he knew what his disciples' reply would be, and yet he asked: "Who do men say that the Son of Man is?"

He wanted his followers—the apostles, the holy women who served him so faithfully, all those who believed in him and accompanied him—sincerely to confront the mystery of his identity. "And they said, 'Some say John the Baptist, others say Elijah, and others Jeremiah or one of the prophets.' "[3]

These praises reflected human admiration for Jesus, esteem for his teaching and deeds (although the Gospels tell us there were negative voices as well). Yet how far they still were from truly knowing him! They seem capable of grasping his greatness, but they fail to discern the mystery of his mission and person. Recognizing the attractiveness of his message, they nevertheless did not perceive him as Savior, the One before whose name (as St. Paul says in the letter to the Philippians) every knee should bend in heaven, on earth, and in hell. The mystery of who Jesus Christ is can only be grasped through the gift of faith, as he himself makes clear in another Gospel passage: "No one comes to me unless he is brought by the Father who sent me."[4] Faith in Christ requires that we pass beyond admiration or appreciation; it requires recognizing our need for conversion and accepting the hand that the Savior lovingly holds out to us.

Let us return to the scene near Caesarea Philippi. Jesus asks: "But who do you say that I am?" Simon Peter, speaking with a supernatural certainty, answers in his own name and that of all of them: "You are the Christ, the son of the living God."[5] His confession recalls words he spoke with similar forcefulness in the synagogue at Capernaum: "You

---

2. Mt 16:13.
3. Mt 16:14.
4. Jn 6:44.
5. Mt 16:16.

have the words of eternal life and we have believed and come to know that you are the Holy One of God."[6]

Both declarations, like so many others in the New Testament, reveal the deep grasp of the mystery of Christ attained by the apostles under the guidance of the Holy Spirit. He is the Messiah, the Son of God and Redeemer of mankind. Today, too, at the start of the third millennium of the redemptive Incarnation, an era in need of a new evangelization, we Christians have to be living witnesses of the mystery of love and salvation that God has revealed to us in Christ. "*Christ is alive.* Jesus, who died on the cross, has risen. He has triumphed over death. He has overcome sorrow, anguish and the power of darkness. . . . He is not someone who has gone, someone who existed for a time and then passed on, leaving us a wonderful example and a great memory. No, Christ is alive. Jesus is the Emmanuel: God with us."[7]

Reason bows before the mystery of filial and fraternal love revealed in him, and the heart expands with the desire to know him better and unite oneself more closely to him. From his plenitude, mankind constantly receives grace upon grace, as St. John wrote in the prologue to his Gospel. The decisive grace is that of being able to follow him closely in our ordinary lives as friends, as brothers and sisters, as faithful Christians, glad to confess: Lord, Son of the living God, we firmly believe in you! You are our Savior and salvation, ground and truth of all reality, ultimate reason for our existence, source of all meaning and value. Only you have words of eternal life!

Reflecting Christ Faithfully and Heroically

To proclaim God's fatherly love and mercy persuasively, our words and deeds must evoke the face of the Redeemer. The life of God's sons and daughters is epitomized in the longing that burned in St. Josemaría's soul: *to know Christ, to make him known, to bring him everywhere.*

---

6. Jn 6:69.
7. St. Josemaría, *Christ Is Passing By*, no. 102.

Here is the core of Christian identity: communion with Christ, and the mission of communicating this precious light to all people and places. God directs this call, this vocation, to all Christians from the moment of Baptism. All the baptized are called to bring the good news of encounter with God with naturalness into their daily encounter with others.

This was well understood by our first brothers and sisters in the faith, who had been taught directly by the apostles or their immediate successors. The *Epistle to Diognetus*, written in the second century, admirably reflects this reality:

> Christians are distinguished from other men neither by country, nor language, nor the customs they observe. For they neither inhabit cities of their own, nor employ a peculiar form of speech, nor lead a life marked out by any singularity. . . . But, inhabiting Greek as well as barbarian cities, according as the lot of each of them has determined, and following the customs of the local people in respect to clothing, food, and the rest of their ordinary conduct, they display to all their wonderful and striking form of life. They dwell in their own countries, but simply as sojourners. As citizens, they share in all things with others, and yet endure all things as if foreigners. Every foreign land is to them as their native country, and every land of their birth as a land of foreigners. They marry, as do the others; they beget children; but they do not destroy their offspring. They have a common table, but not a common bed. They are in the flesh, but they do not live after the flesh. They pass their days on earth, but are citizens of heaven.[8]

The effort to reflect Christ can sometimes startle those around us and even become a "sign of contradiction." In the Temple at Jerusalem Simeon foretold that Jesus himself would become for many a "sign that is spoken against." So, too, the first disciples when, having received the Holy Spirit, they rushed forth to give witness to Jesus. At first they were taken for drunk; then they were imprisoned; finally they were

---

8. *Epistle to Diognetus*, V, 1–9.

condemned to death. The spread of the Christian message in the world went hand in hand with the witness of many men and women prepared to put faithfulness to the Master before a tranquil life, honor, fortune, and social status. From the early martyrs until now, much blood has flowed along with the Blood shed by Jesus on the Cross to save us.

The ancient document just cited tells us that Christians "obey the prescribed laws, but their lives surpass the laws. They love all men, and are persecuted by all. They are unknown and condemned; they are put to death, and restored to life . . . they are dishonored, and yet in their very dishonor are glorified. They are slandered, and yet are justified; they are reviled, and bless; they are insulted, and repay the insult with honor; they do good, yet are punished as evildoers. Condemned to death, they rejoice as if they were being given life."[9]

With God's grace, this heroism will be present among Christians until the end of the world. The devil will never cease persecuting those who seek to offer coherent witness to Christ, but our Lord wants his followers to remain faithful, determined not to let their identity be dimmed by persecution or pressure from cultures opposed to Christ's transforming message.

St. Josemaría insisted that "a Christian's faith has nothing whatever to do with conformity, inertia or lack of initiative."[10] How sad it is when Christians hide their faith, or set it aside at work, at the office or university, in business or politics, in social life or in the communication media. One thinks of St. Thomas More who, while remaining a faithful citizen, was ready to give testimony to his faith even at the cost of his life.

Jesus asks his followers to spread his message throughout the world, with the strength and optimism that come from knowing his teaching to be ever timely, ever new with the timelessness of love. St. Josemaría suggested that each day we ask ourselves: "Do I spread Christian life to those around me?"[11]

---

9. Ibid., 10–16.
10. *Christ Is Passing By*, no. 42.
11. St. Josemaría, *The Forge*, no. 856.

Confronting this question can help one overcome the danger, ever present but especially so in times of cultural change, of yielding to pressure and separating one's private life from one's social and professional lives. To do that would mean being unfaithful to the truth and preferring "political correctness" that challenges no one—not because it is nourished by understanding and charity (as should always be the case), but because it lacks substance and produces (at best) a façade of respectability.

To Reflect Christ, To Know Christ

Christ continues today the redemptive mission he received from the Father. As he began to preach, Jesus applied to himself words from the prophet Isaiah: "The Spirit of the Lord is upon me, because he has anointed me to preach good news to the poor. He has sent me to proclaim release to the captives and recovering of sight to the blind, to set at liberty those who are oppressed, to proclaim the acceptable year of the Lord."[12] The same Spirit, flowing from Christ's Cross, is given to the Church of all times.

Jesus Christ came to save us. Consider some of the Gospel scenes that make this clear. St. Joseph is told in a dream: "You shall call his name Jesus, for he will save his people from their sins."[13] An angel announces to the shepherds: "For to you is born this day in the city of David a Savior, who is Christ the Lord."[14] John the Baptist, the precursor, recognizes Jesus as "the Lamb of God who takes away the sin of the world."[15] Years later, the apostle Peter exhorts Christians always to grow "in the knowledge of our Lord and Savior Jesus Christ,"[16] and Paul urges Christians to live soberly and devoutly in this world, awaiting the manifestation "of our great God and Savior Jesus Christ."[17]

---

12. Lk 4:18–19.
13. Mt 1:21.
14. Lk 2:11.
15. Jn 1:29.
16. 2 Pet 3:18.
17. Tit 2:13.

Only Jesus is Savior. The Church proclaims this, and we should pass on the good news to everyone we meet, helping them, as St. Paul says, "to know the love of Christ which surpasses all knowledge."[18] The word "know" here refers not only to intellectual knowledge but to knowledge assimilated in prayer that blazes in our hearts and shapes our deeds. We must announce Christ by the way we live, being to those around us "Christ who is passing by." Or, more precisely, trying to be that, for we are weak and have many failings. St. Josemaría tells us always to strive "that our thoughts be sincere, full of peace, self-giving and service . . . that we be true and clear in what we say—the right thing at the right time—so as to console and help and especially bring God's light to others. Let us pray that our actions be consistent and effective and right, so that they give off *the good fragrance of Christ* (2 Cor 2:15), evoking his way of doing things."[19]

Everything in Christ's life manifests the divine life. As St. Paul says, "In him the whole fullness of deity dwells bodily."[20] We should meditate deeply on our Lord's life and, in the first place, on the mystery of the Cross. On the summit of Calvary, the Cross held in its arms the Redeemer's body, showing us the magnitude of God's love. The Child in Bethlehem also offers us abundant lessons. And the years Jesus spent growing up and working alongside Joseph are filled with significance. St. Josemaría wrote: "The fact that Jesus grew up and lived just like us shows us that human existence and all our daily, ordinary activities have a divine meaning."[21]

Christians have the noble mission of showing Jesus Christ to our fellow men and women, some by preaching, others by the testimony of consecrated lives; but the great multitude of Christians, called to seek holiness in the middle of the world, must make the Master known by doing their work and fulfilling their other duties well, with human excellence and a Christian spirit.

---

18. Eph 3:19.

19. *Christ Is Passing By*, no. 156.

20. Col 2:9.

21. *Christ Is Passing By*, no. 14; see also St. Josemaría, *Friends of God*, no. 56.

"Christ our Lord,"— and once again I quote St. Josemaría—"was crucified; from the height of the Cross, he redeemed the world, thereby restoring peace between God and mankind. Jesus reminds all of us: *et ego, si exaltatus fuero a terra, omnia traham ad meipsum.* 'And I, if I be lifted up from the earth, I will draw all things to myself' (Jn 12:32). If you put me at the center of all the earthly activities, he is saying, by fulfilling the duty of each moment, in what appears important and what appears unimportant, *omnia traham ad meipsum,* I will draw everything to myself. My kingdom among you will be a reality! . . . Embracing the Christian faith means committing oneself to continuing Jesus Christ's mission among men. We must, each of us, be *alter Christus, ipse Christus,* another Christ, Christ himself. Only in this way can we set about this great undertaking, this immense, unending task of sanctifying all temporal structures from within, bringing to them the leaven of redemption."[22]

This is the path: getting to know the Master, identifying with him, having him always with us. Made Christ-bearers through grace, we can make him known by our words and our lives as God's children.

---

22. *Christ Is Passing By*, no. 183.

The Holy Spirit:
Love Leading Us to Love

"Come, Father of the poor; come, Giver of all graces, come, Light of our hearts." The liturgy prays this prayer on the solemnity of Pentecost, singing the glory of the Holy Spirit and the richness of his gifts.

But the prayer expresses not only God's infinite greatness, but also our human needs and our yearning for unending life and joy. The linking of God's immense riches and our own poverty contains an important lesson: to raise our eyes above our human indigence, not seeing it as a barrier between God and his creatures. God is not distant from us up in heaven where all is splendor and joy, while here on earth we have suffering and troubles. Each of us comes from the loving hands of our Father God, who sent his Son into the world to save us, and poured forth his Spirit to enlighten and guide us on the path that leads to him.

The gesture of divine love recounted in the Genesis telling of man's creation is renewed in each of us. God looks on us with that same special love with which he regarded the inanimate figure, made of mud from the earth, into which he breathed the "breath of life." He infused into human beings a spirit that comes from him and permits us to aspire to another life, a sharing in the divine nature of the Most Blessed Trinity.

After the fall of our first parents, God did not stop loving us. He renewed and strengthened his love; and once the Redemption was accomplished, he sent us from the Cross of Christ his Spirit, his own Love. Through Baptism and Confirmation, the marvelous reality of the first day of Pentecost is reenacted in our own souls. "For we ourselves," we read in one of the Apostle's letters, "were once foolish, disobedient, led astray . . . but when the goodness and loving kindness of God our Savior appeared, he saved us, not because of deeds done by us in righteousness, but in virtue of his own mercy, by the washing of regeneration and renewal in the Holy Spirit, which he poured out upon us richly through Jesus Christ our Savior."[1]

From the time we are baptized, an event both simple and great, the Holy Spirit begins to act in us, impelling us to lead lives that mirror the life of Christ Jesus. True, as tiny children we could not reason and give thanks for his supernatural action at work in us. But let us give thanks now, having grown in years and in the faith. Let us respond generously to the action of the Spirit, who makes us children of the Father in the Son.

The Gift of the Holy Spirit

The apostle St. John wrote: "God is Love."[2] These words, full of light and fire, sum up all of Christ's revelation, and provide us with the best preamble to any meditation on the Holy Spirit.

To grasp their content more fully, recall how the Apostle introduces them: "He who does not love does not know God." Loving is an indispensable condition for knowing this God who is Love.

The Holy Spirit is revealed to us within the Blessed Trinity as the eternal Love with which the Father and the Son love each other. In St. Augustine's expression, the Spirit is the ineffable communion

---

1. Tit. 3:3–6.
2. 1 Jn. 4:8.

between Father and Son, the *nexus* between the first two Persons of the Trinity. Human language is incapable of expressing the intensity and depth of this communion. But through grace, Augustine insists, "this ineffable embrace of the Father and his Image . . . is given with infinite liberality and abundance to all mankind."[3] Through the action of the Spirit in our souls, we receive what our own powers could never attain: knowledge of God and his Love, communion with the Three Divine Persons.

"If a man loves me," Jesus said in the long, intimate conversation with his disciples at the Last Supper, "he will keep my word, and my Father will love him, and we will come to him and make our home with him."[4] This is the sublime mystery that takes place in a soul in grace. Pope John Paul II called it "the greatest and holiest reality in Christian spirituality."[5] The Most Holy Trinity, Father and Son with the Spirit of Love who unites them, dwells in the souls of those who live in accord with Christ's word. He acts in our faculties, guides our thoughts, confers strength on our efforts, elevates our affections. If we accept this gift and open ourselves freely to divine grace, we are divinized. Under the Paraclete's action, all our acts, great or small, become manifestations of love for God and our fellow men and women.

In the Trinity's self-giving to creatures, the Holy Spirit, the first gift and source of all other gifts, marks God's action in the world—in history, in the life of the Church, in each soul—with the imprint of love. This love, as Dante sang, is what moves not only human hearts but also "the sun and all the stars."[6] It draws together and unifies everything. If we consider that the Holy Spirit is, in the Trinity's life, the bond uniting Father and Son, we see why unity is one of the clearest reflections in us of God's love: unity in our personal life, consistency in what we do with the faith we profess, unity in the Church, unity with all mankind expressed in deeds.

---

3. *On the Trinity*, VI, 10, 11.
4. Jn. 14:23.
5. John Paul II, *Address at a general audience*, September 2, 1990.
6. *Divine Comedy, Paradise*, canto 33.

Love for unity brings with it a universal spirit, an openness of mind and heart. It is an important part of what humankind, torn apart by divisions and separations of all kinds, expects of Christians today. And here too the Holy Spirit is God's gift, a gift the world badly needs. Drawing close to the third Person of the Trinity does not distance us from others but gives us the perspective we need to grasp the true meaning of history and mankind's deepest aspirations and sentiments; taking up our daily tasks with new strength, we do all we can to help solve the pressing problems of the world.

Jesus promised his followers: "It is to your advantage that I go away, for if I do not go away, the Paraclete will not come to you; but if I go, I will send him to you."[7] The coming of the Holy Spirit, who is the Consoler (that is what the Greek term *Paracletos* means), crowns God's plan of creation and redemption. He brings Christ's mission to completion and opens a dialogue between God and mankind that will never end.

Docility to the Holy Spirit

The love the Holy Spirit infuses into our hearts—a love for which we have been created and in which we find happiness—fosters an authentic way of loving: not a superficial, passing sentiment, but generous self-giving shown in deeds. This is the core of Christian life, as Pope John Paul II frequently recalled, citing Vatican Council II: "Man, who is the only creature on earth that God willed for itself, cannot fully find himself except through a sincere gift of himself."[8]

God gave himself for us and wants us to give ourselves back to him. To each of us he speaks the words of St. Paul to the faithful at Corinth: "For I seek not what is yours but you."[9] St. Josemaría said: "Jesus isn't satisfied with 'sharing': he wants everything."[10] This ideal may be a bit

---

7. Jn. 16:7.
8. Vatican II, Const. *Gaudium et Spes*, 24.
9. 2 Cor. 12:14.
10. *The Way*, no. 155.

unsettling at first; but aware that the God who asks for our self-giving has also made it possible by his gifts, especially the gift of himself, we know that converting our life into an offering pleasing to God is truly within our reach.

The grace granted to us through the outpouring of the Holy Spirit enables us to love God unreservedly, with the love that is a sharing in the love of God the Father, who has loved us to the point of sending his Son to become man and shed his blood for us.

When, moved by the Holy Spirit, we have arranged our whole existence according to the demands of love, what God asks of us is no longer seen as renunciation or burden, but as a series of opportunities to find God and become more closely united with him. Christian maturity is attained by the victory of love, which overcomes fear and selfishness.

But there is no victory in the spiritual life without a struggle—and this struggle will last our whole life. Attachments, a worldly viewpoint, distraction by momentary satisfactions, the assertion of ego, all make it hard for us to open our hearts to God's loving plans. Yet the Paraclete urges us constantly ahead along the path of spiritual growth, and docility to his inspirations is all that we need.

Whoever seeks to do as the Holy Spirit indicates can count on his help. What seemed impossible becomes attainable, what seemed hard becomes a point of departure for a still more generous response. A liturgical hymn invokes the Paraclete as "the soul's most welcome guest;/ Sweet refreshment here below;/ In our labor, rest most sweet;/ Grateful coolness in the heat;/ Solace in the midst of woe."[11] The Spirit consoles us in suffering, protects us in danger, comforts us in grief, strengthens us in trials.

Theologians sometimes have used the image of a boat to describe the role of the Holy Spirit in Christian life. The supernatural virtues made present in our soul by Baptism are the oars, which require effort

---

11. Sequence *Veni, Sancte Spiritus,* from the Mass of Pentecost.

and cause fatigue. The gifts of the Holy Spirit are the sails, driven forward by the wind. The way of Christian sanctity is a joyful battle directed to conquering the residue of sin. But at every moment God the Holy Spirit inspires us and sustains us, and, if it is good for us, makes us feel his consolations.

The action of the Paraclete is gentle, discreet. It does not eliminate our freedom but presupposes it. When we cooperate, it reveals all its divine power. Scripture uses the image of wind for the Spirit's intervention: sometimes impetuous, sometimes gentle, always active and efficacious. It also uses the image of a fire that burns and purifies, and of water that springs up to everlasting life. These images should awaken in us a firm hope and trust in God.

The first letter of St. John says: "For this is the love of God, that we keep his commandments. And his commandments are not burdensome."[12] Someone might be tempted to find here an insoluble paradox: doesn't linking love to the fulfillment of specific commandments negate love's spontaneity? Another Scripture passage, from the book of Ezekiel, holds the answer: "A new heart I will give you, and a new spirit I will put within you; and I will take out of your flesh the heart of stone and give you a heart of flesh. And I will put my spirit within you, and cause you to walk in my statutes and be careful to observe my ordinances."[13]

The Church's Tradition has seen here a promise of the gift of the Holy Spirit. God sends love because he is Love. Created in his image, we are made for love. He sent us his Son to show us how great his love is; and now he continues to send the Holy Spirit into our hearts, to divinize us and make it possible for us to share in God's own love.

In his dialogue with the Samaritan woman at the well of Sichar, Jesus confronted her objections to his invitation to drink of "living water"—in other words, to open herself to the grace of the Holy Spirit.

---

12. 1 Jn 5:3.
13. Ezek 36:26–27.

This meant for her a radical change of behavior, a deep conversion, after having plunged her heart into many fetid puddles. But our Lord exclaims: "If you knew the gift of God. . . . "[14] St. Augustine, in his treatise on the Trinity, notes that "gift" is a proper name of the Holy Spirit. He is the gift of God the Father to the Son and of the Son to the Father, and source of all God's gifts to us. If we knew the gift of God! If we were aware of God's power present in us thanks to the sending of the Holy Spirit, we would realize how God, by his grace, enables us to reach goals that we in our weakness imagine to be unattainable.

Many souls turn their backs on the marvelous adventure of sanctity due to discouragement and mistrust! In contrast, wonderful fruit comes from hope—from determination to seek in the Spirit the power that we lack! The gift of the Spirit, which blows where and how it wills, is communicated especially through the channels of grace, the sacraments, which Jesus entrusted to the Church and in which he acts with sovereign power as Lord. Here our paths on earth intersect with the pathways of God. Let us travel along them with faith, loving the Church. And so we shall receive the Holy Spirit.

---

14. Jn 4:10.

Mary Most Holy:
Mother of God and Our Mother

Holiness is always marked by magnanimity—the generous desire to share one's riches and gifts with others. God, infinitely holy and magnanimous, wishes us to share in his life, granting us his grace and raising us to the supernatural order. To help us attain such immense happiness, he decreed—among other unmistakable signs of his love—that we be under the protection of the woman who brought Christ into this world: the Blessed Virgin Mary, Mother of God and our Mother.

The Incarnation impresses a deep Marian imprint on everything Christian. It is a fundamental element of our faith. Mary's central role in the economy of salvation was determined by God in choosing her to be the Mother of his Incarnate Son, who later, at the foot of the Cross, entrusted to her the care of each of us.

The supernatural gifts that embellish her and enable her to carry out her mission in the history of salvation next to Christ are a bright light guiding us on our way. Her daily acts of service in Nazareth, living with her Son and St. Joseph; her fidelity at the dreadful moment of Jesus' Passion and in the hours before the Resurrection; her refined presence during the first steps of the Christian community constitute matter for our constant meditation. Even her slightest gestures tell us of her ardent love for God's will.

Christian tradition testifies eloquently to the meaning of Mary. But we are still far from grasping all of our Lady's spiritual dignity and greatness. The Church venerates her with filial affection as Mother most lovable—a model of faith, hope, charity, and all the other virtues. We too should nourish our "personal experience of Mary's maternal love,"[1] which, as St. Josemaría often said, leads us straight to an encounter with the love of God the Father, God the Son, and God the Holy Spirit.

Mary's Greatness

In his encyclical *Redemptoris Mater*, Pope John Paul II sums up the core of Catholic faith regarding Mary: "By virtue of the richness of the grace of the beloved Son, by reason of the redemptive merits of him who willed to become her Son, Mary was preserved from the inheritance of original sin. In this way, from the first moment of her conception— which is to say, of her existence—she belonged to Christ, sharing in the salvific and sanctifying grace and in that love which has its beginning in the 'Beloved,' the Son of the Eternal Father, who through the Incarnation became her own Son."[2]

Filled with heavenly gifts, raised above the angels and the saints, Mary possesses an innocence and sanctity beyond the comprehension of created intellects. We, her children, contemplate in her a majesty and dignity that go hand in hand with great tenderness and simplicity. "We know," said St. Josemaría, "that it is a divine secret,"[3] but a secret that makes us fall in love and therefore gives us great joy.

This "divine secret" is foretold in the first pages of Genesis. After the original sin, God announces that he will put enmity between the

---

1. Cf. *Friends of God*, no. 293.
2. John Paul II, Encyclical *Redemptoris Mater*, no. 10.
3. *Christ Is Passing By*, no. 171.

serpent and the woman. The greeting of Gabriel, angel of the Annunciation, to that young girl who from all eternity was the beloved daughter in the Beloved Son set this process in motion: "Hail Mary, full of grace, the Lord is with you."[4] Thus, with great simplicity, the message of salvation is spoken. The Trinity's plan for our Redemption, whereby we share as sons and daughters in divine life, enters upon its time of culmination. Even as the angel's words resonated in Mary's heart, God's purposes began to be realized out in history.

The sanctity of this woman, conceived without sin and faithful at every step along her way, discloses the refinement of God's love and the marvels accessible to human freedom when a soul decides to be faithful. Our Lady is the Blessed Trinity's "masterwork,"[5] as the *Catechism of the Catholic Church* says, and our best model for following Christ. Mary precedes us and immeasurably surpasses us; yet this humble handmaid of Nazareth, "espoused to a man named Joseph, of the house of David," also encourages us to imitate her. Christians are called to draw close to Christ by drawing close to Mary.

Through her too, God asks us to take part generously in the work entrusted to the Church by his Son, born of the Virgin Mary. We are to cooperate with faith, hope, and charity in restoring supernatural life to souls and spreading the Gospel message of peace and joy, of salvation, through the world. We are chosen from eternity to be holy and lead others to holiness—to be Christ-bearers like her and a leaven of holiness in the middle of the world.

Great Holiness in Everyday Life

The lesson of Mary's life, as St. Josemaría said, is that sanctity doesn't require spectacular deeds. It lies "in the hidden and silent sacrifice of each day. . . . To become Godlike, to be divinized, we must begin by being very human, accepting from God our condition as ordinary

4. Lk 1:28.
5. *Catechism of the Catholic Church*, no. 721.

men and women and sanctifying its apparent unimportance. Thus did Mary live. She who is full of grace, the object of God's pleasure, exalted above all the angels and the saints, lived an ordinary life."[6]

Here is one of the essential features of our Lady's earthly existence and of the model of holiness she offers. In the home of Jesus, Mary, and Joseph in Nazareth a visitor learns that whoever seeks to serve and please God can find him in ordinary life. Mary's life is evidence that one can be fully immersed in daily activities while at the same time diviniz-ing them. We can be "contemplatives in the middle of the world."

And if the magnitude of this ideal seems daunting, one can draw strength from the example of our Lady's faithful response as well as her constant help. For she reigns alongside her Son in heaven and is always ready to extend to us her maternal affection and care. Indeed, she comes to our help even before we ask, though often her loving pro-tection goes unnoticed by us.

Our Lady's path, like her Son's, does not turn away from the Cross. The significance of the salvific Cross—suffering accepted with faith and love in the work of salvation—is a central element of the Christian vocation. It was therefore central in the life of our Lady, whose soul was pierced by a sword as the aged Simeon prophesied. It is a mistake to fear the Cross. Someone who does as Mary did is certain to experience the joy that floods the soul of one who forgets about self and trusts in Jesus' redeeming love. Mary's maternal love, lived to the fullest extent possible beside her Son on Calvary, extends a powerful yet gentle invi-tation to share in her self-surrender for the world's salvation.

Jesus told his disciples to "take up their daily cross and follow me."[7] Deep understanding of the Christian meaning of the Cross is a grace that sheds light on all of our days, and especially when life seems hard or even absurd. But the Cross also illuminates everyday life with its small annoyances.

---

6. *Christ Is Passing By*, no. 172.
7. Cf. Lk 9:23.

The treasure of the Cross is found in the daily effort to understand others and treat them generously, in the small, everyday opportunities for service in family, work, and social life. It is present in the joyful testimony of temperance, love for holy purity, solidarity with the suffering and needy. We find the Cross also in avoiding every occasion of sin, fleeing from temptation, and returning quickly to God through sacramental confession.

Mary, Daughter of God the Father, Mother of God the Son, Spouse and Temple of God the Holy Spirit, goes before us on the path of faithfully following Jesus. The road to sanctity, the struggle to imitate and identify ourselves with Christ, lies along the path of love for our Lady and filial conversation with her. As Bishop Alvaro del Portillo, my predecessor as Prelate of Opus Dei liked to say, we should go to Mary "in everything and for everything."

Filled with trust and knowing well our personal weakness, we tell her: "My mother . . . may your love bind me to your Son's Cross: may I lack neither the faith nor the courage to do the will of our Jesus."[8]

---

8. *The Way,* no. 497.

CHAPTER
5

Love for the Church, Responsibility in the Church

"*Et unam, sanctam, catholicam et apostolicam Ecclesiam!* I can well understand that pause of yours as you pray, savoring the words: 'I believe in the Church, One, Holy, Catholic and Apostolic'"; and also: "What joy to be able to say with all the fervor of my soul: I love my Mother, the holy Church!"[1] These words from *The Way* highlight the deep Christian conviction that one is never a Christian in isolation. Faith is always lived in and through the Church.

There are abundant witnesses to this conviction down through the centuries. But let us go directly to the most recent ecumenical Council, Vatican II, where the Magisterium expressed the reality of this mystery with special clarity and depth.

The Mystery of the Church, Mother and Home of Christians

The Council, in the constitution *Lumen Gentium*, focused on the mystery of the Church. The Church, it said, is much more than a human

1. *The Way*, nos. 517 and 518.

institution, more than just the assembly of those who, in sharing the same faith, continue a tradition born twenty centuries ago. The Church is made up of men and women, but it comes from God. Christ, the Son of God made man, called the first disciples and sent them to preach the Gospel to the entire world. He expressly promised, in words recorded by St. Matthew: "I am with you always, to the close of the age."[2] Together with the Father, he sends the Holy Spirit, who acts in the soul of every Christian from the moment of Baptism and assists the Church's shepherds, building up the ecclesial community and guiding it, by preserving the Church in the truth and communicating life to it.

The Council echoed St. Cyprian in calling the Church "a people brought into unity from the unity of the Father, the Son and the Holy Spirit."[3] Transcending our human strength and weaknesses, the Church lives by divine charity, by God's life and strength: by the love of the Father, who constantly draws her towards himself; by the love of the Son, who is always present with his infinite redemptive power; by the love of the Holy Spirit, who seeks continually to stir up faith, hope, and charity in every heart.

"A people brought into unity from the unity of the Father, the Son and the Holy Spirit." Consider these words of the great bishop of Carthage. We are Christians as a result of God's unceasing salvific action. The Church, born of divine grace, is both instrument and sacrament, used by God to communicate his grace. We are born in the Church as Christians by Baptism, strengthened by Confirmation, nourished by the Eucharist, reconciled with God by Penance. In the Church we hear the Gospel and are taught to walk according to God's will.

The Church, Spouse of Jesus Christ, reflects God's goodness and holiness, as Christian tradition has affirmed from the days of St. Paul. It is God who acts in the Church and through the Church. The Christian's spontaneous attitude toward the Church is love, sincere and deep, filial, filled with trust and gratitude. A Christian should never speak of

---

2. Mt 28:20.

3. St. Cyprian, cited in Dogmatic Constitution *Lumen Gentium*, no. 4.

the Church with indifference or coldness. We speak of our Mother the Church with deep interest and affection, as someone does in speaking of something holy that is central to his or her life.

Christians are human beings and therefore capable of evil and sin. All eras in the Church's history have been marked by the inevitable consequences of human weakness. But that does not call into question the holiness of the Church. For God is at work at every moment to preserve the holiness of the one Church despite human weaknesses.

St. Josemaría, speaking of the falls and weaknesses of Christians, said. "All this is true, but it does not authorize us in any way to judge the Church in a human manner, without theological faith. We cannot consider only the greater or lesser merits of certain churchmen or of some Christians. To do so would be to limit ourselves to the surface of things. What is most important in the Church is not how we humans react but how God acts. This is what the Church is: Christ present in our midst, God coming toward men in order to save them, calling us with his revelation, sanctifying us with his grace, maintaining us with his constant help, in the great and small battles of our daily life."[4]

Christ's presence in the Church should provoke in us a sincere love for such a good Mother—love shown in words and deeds. In receiving Christian life from the Church we are incorporated into Christ's Mystical Body and called to share in its mission, transmitting to others the life we have received. Thus we help spread the Gospel to new generations who receive the faith and in their turn become part of Christ's Body, his One, Holy, Catholic, and Apostolic Church.

The Second Vatican Council made it clear that all Catholics, not just some, have been called in Baptism to follow Christ and cooperate in his mission. "The state of this people" says *Lumen Gentium*, "is that of the dignity and freedom of the sons of God . . . Its law is the new commandment to love as Christ loved us (cf. Jn 13:34). Its destiny is the kingdom of God which has been begun by God himself on earth

---

4. *Christ Is Passing By*, no. 131.

and which is to be further extended until it is brought to perfection by him at the end of time, when Christ our life will appear."[5] Therefore, we read in the decree *Apostolicam Actuositatem*, the Christian vocation "by its very nature is also a vocation to the apostolate. No part of the structure of a living body is merely passive but has a share in the functions as well as life of the body. The same is true for the Body of Christ, the Church: 'the whole body achieves full growth in dependence on the full functioning of each part' (Eph 4:16)."[6]

All the baptized have received the mission of proclaiming Christ, making him known by their words and conduct. This is so much the case that those who did not strive to be apostles couldn't claim altogether truthfully to be Christians. Just as in Christ it is impossible to separate his being the God-Man from his role as Redeemer, so, said St. Josemaría, it is not possible to separate a Christian's call to divine intimacy from the responsibility of bringing others to our Lord, to share in his riches.

Love for the Church and Union with the Pope and the Bishops

Since at least the third century, the Mass of the Latin liturgy has contained a prayer for the Roman Pontiff and the local bishop. The unity of the Church, expressed and made real in an eminent way in the Eucharist, necessarily includes communion with the Pope and the bishops. Our Lord established his Church as a structured community with a diversity of ministries and charisms. In particular, as an essential part of that structure he established the episcopal ministry and the college of bishops. The head of these successors to the apostles is the Bishop of Rome, St. Peter's successor. The apostolic continuity instituted by Jesus Christ reaches back in an uninterrupted chain to the first Twelve and is the grounding of the authority of the Pope and the bishops.

---

5. *Lumen Gentium*, no. 9.
6. Decree *Apostolicam Actuositatem*, no. 2.

Bishops receive from Christ the fullness of the Sacrament of Holy Orders. The bishop of each portion of the People of God is the visible foundation of its unity and the one chiefly responsible for building up the faithful in Christ with the cooperation of priests and deacons. He has the mission of announcing the Gospel in the name of and on behalf of Christ. He is the administrator of grace, above all in the Eucharistic action performed by himself or the priests in communion with him. As Christ's vicar, each bishop also has the task of governing the community entrusted to him, fostering by his exhortation, counsel, and mandate apostolic zeal and the desire for holiness.

The Bishop of Rome, the Roman Pontiff, is head of the College of Bishops and pastor of the universal Church. He is the common father of all Christians, the rock guaranteeing the faithful continuity of the Church in the truth of the Gospel. As the Second Vatican Council said, the Pope is "the perpetual and visible source and foundation of the unity both of the bishops and of the whole company of the faithful."[7]

The Pope and the other bishops are called to pour themselves out for the needs of the faithful, taking as their inspiration the words of St. Paul: "Who is weak, and I am not weak? Who is made to fall, and I am not indignant?"[8] Like the Good Shepherd of the parable, they do not behave like hirelings who flee at the moments of danger and abandon the flock but like true shepherds who give their life for their sheep.[9]

If a single word defines the spirit of ecclesial ministry, and especially the episcopal ministry, it is service. In the first place, service to Christ, to his Person, to his teaching and sacraments, since shepherds in the Church are not meant to speak about themselves but to echo Christ's words faithfully and tend the channels by which grace and life come to his flock, in this way serving also their brothers and sisters in the faith, whom our Lord has entrusted to their care.

---

7. *Lumen Gentium*, no. 23.
8. 2 Cor 11:29.
9. Cf. Jn 10:11–13.

The authority of pastors in the Church is comprehensible only in the context of obedience to a mandate received from Jesus Christ. It carries with it a function and position received gratuitously, as gift and exalted task, together with the command that they be exercised for the benefit of others. This requires on the pastors' part forgetfulness of self and dedication to the Christian community; and on the part of the faithful, gratitude for all that Christ has given the Church to open up the path of sanctity. To heed the ecclesiastical hierarchy means heeding Christ, who speaks through his representatives. To love it means loving Christ, present through his ministers.

All the baptized have received the common priesthood of the faithful, in virtue of which they are called to share in Christ's mission. They do this in their own specific ways, according to their personal vocations. In all cases, however, they must act in close union with the shepherds, who through the Sacrament of Orders have received the ministerial priesthood.

Appreciation for the mystery of the Church increases love for her and gives us the desire to serve her as loyal sons and daughters. Recognizing the divine plan underlying the ministry of the Pope and the other bishops similarly moves one to give thanks to God for the means divine providence provides to ensure fidelity of faith and moral rectitude in conduct. With firm faith and unwavering charity, Catholics must maintain the bonds of unity in the Church by their heartfelt adherence to the Pope and the bishops in communion with him. Filial affection for the Roman Pontiff leads them to love and pray for all the bishops in the world.

St. Josemaría liked to pray: *Omnes cum Petro, ad Iesum per Mariam.* United to Peter and the Church, protected by the powerful intercession of Mary, we come to Jesus, the Love of our loves, bringing all mankind with us.

PART II

COMING TO KNOW GOD

CHAPTER

6

Conversion, Beginning of the Christian Path

"Behold, I send my messenger before thy face, who shall prepare thy way; the voice of one crying in the wilderness: 'Prepare the way of the Lord, make his paths straight.'"[1] These words of the prophet Isaiah, applied to John the Baptist, open the Gospel of St. Mark.

Here is an opportunity to enter into the Gospel "as another character in the scene,"[2] just as the founder of Opus Dei recommends: "You will find the Life of Jesus, but you should also find your own life there."[3]

Reading and meditating on Mark's Gospel during successive Sundays of ordinary time, one accompanies Christ along the roads of Palestine. One witnesses his great miracles and hears him teach with authority, leading those present to exclaim, "We never saw anything like this!"[4] At other moments, one feels his reproach to his disciples:

---

1. Mk 1:2–3.
2. Cf. *The Forge*, no. 8.
3. Ibid., no. 754.
4. Mk 2:12.

"Have you no faith?"[5] This comes as a rebuke to us, slow as we are to understand our Lord's words.

With the confidence of knowing ourselves part of the intimate circle of our Lord's disciples, we dare to speak up, telling him—as they did—all our concerns: our projects, our fatigue, our lack of faithfulness, our joys. We unite ourselves eagerly to Peter's confession: "You are the Christ."[6] And later, our redemption having been accomplished, we are carried away by the sorrow and faith of the centurion and exclaim: "Truly this man was the Son of God!"[7] Finally, with joy and humility, we receive with the Eleven the mandate of the risen Lord: "Go into all the world and preach the gospel to the whole creation."[8]

The Gospel, A Call to Conversion

St. Mark's narrative begins with the preaching of John the Baptist, preparing our Lord's way with a summons to "a baptism of repentance for the forgiveness of sins."[9] The Precursor's exhortation is continued and perfected by Christ as he begins his own preaching: "The time is fulfilled, and the kingdom of God is at hand; repent, and believe in the gospel."[10] But Jesus adds something of singular importance: "Believe in the Gospel"—that is, open your minds and hearts to the good news I bring. The first step remains the same: convert, change your heart, recognize your need for transformation in the depths of your being.

The call to conversion at the start of Christ's public life was not due to any special problems that Christ's contemporaries raised to his message. The men and women of those times had defects and virtues

---

5. Mk 4:40.
6. Mk 8:29.
7. Mk 15:39.
8. Mk 16:15.
9. Mk 1:4.
10. Mk 1:15.

just as we do. We too need to alter our conduct in order to hear God's call. Christ's words, though spoken two thousand years ago, were not addressed only to that generation. They have the same power and timeliness now. As Pope John Paul II said: "The whole of human history in fact stands in reference to him: our own time and the future of the world are illumined by his presence."[11]

Why did Jesus begin by stressing the need for conversion? Why does the Church down through the centuries issue the same call? The answer is in Christ's words: The kingdom of God is at hand, the manifestation of God's sovereign, loving power is imminent. We need conversion to ready us to receive Jesus, our Savior, the Son sent by the Father who will free us from evil and sin and, having sent us the Holy Spirit, will lead us to full intimacy with the Blessed Trinity. Our Lord is knocking at the door of our hearts, and we, knowing ourselves to be "nothing and less than nothing,"[12] need to undergo an inner transformation, rooted in a deep act of humility by which we place ourselves trustingly in God's hands. Then his grace can purify us and draw us into communion with him.

Christ's call to repentance still resounds today. "Jesus is the genuine newness which surpasses all human expectations and such he remains for ever, from age to age."[13] Therefore the Church must repeat his invitation to conversion. For some it may be the first, for others, one of many that have already taken place. However that may be, each of us should respond with honest determination, for constant interior renewal is essential to perseverance in following Christ—in loving him ever more and better.

Using a strong and expressive phrase, St. Paul says: "The day of the Lord will come like a thief in the night."[14] This is not meant to alarm us but to awaken us to the need to be watchful. The words refer directly

---

11. Bull of Indiction *Incarnationis Mysterium*, November 29, 1998, no. 1.

12. St. Josemaría, *The Way*, no. 432.

13. *Incarnationis Mysterium*, no. 1.

14. 1 Thess 5:2.

to our Lord's coming in glory at the end of time, but they also point to a reality repeated in the personal history of each soul. The "day of the Lord" comes not only at the moment of death or in special situations obliging one to reflect more deeply on the meaning of life; it comes also in daily events. Christ constantly is passing by, and we must constantly be alert to his voice.

Jesus invites each of us to a personal encounter with God, who alone can satisfy the deepest longings of the human heart. This is why one must face each day's events with joy, aware of their divine meaning. To share in the wedding feast, however, requires the proper attire. In Christ's parable about the wedding feast, the guest who was not wearing a nuptial garment is expelled from the celebration.

Conversion involves struggling to free oneself from obstacles on the path to God, from sin, and to don the wedding garment—that is, to follow the new commandment of love—unreservedly. This is not an easy thing to do. For one's soul still harbors dark corners of selfishness and vanity that must be washed clean. Like the prodigal son, we have more often wasted our inheritance—God's gifts—and, acknowledging that fact, we need to retrace our steps and return to the house of our Father God.

Conversion and Life

But let us return to St. Mark's Gospel. John the Baptist not only exhorts but baptizes, with a rite that moves people to desire conversion. Although his baptism contained an invitation to penance, however, it did not grant the gifts of the Messiah. John was a figure of what was to come, as the Baptist himself declared: "After me comes he who is mightier than I, the thong of whose sandals I am not worthy to stoop down and untie. I have baptized you with water; but he will baptize you with the Holy Spirit."[15]

The Baptism of Jesus, which we Christians receive, is a baptism not only with water, but with water and the Spirit: it removes sin and

---

15. Mk 1:7–8.

confers supernatural life. And as if this great gift were not enough, we are also offered what some Fathers of the Church called the "second tablet of salvation"—the Sacrament of Penance and Reconciliation. Jesus, speaking through the priest's words of absolution, stanches our wounds. In Baptism and in Penance we encounter Jesus who saves, Jesus who cures, Jesus who pardons, Jesus who loves. And, as a fruit of this encounter, we have within us the Holy Spirit, empowering us to persevere and to live as conversion implies.

We also share in the marvelous reality of the Communion of Saints. The spiritual struggle is not carried on in isolation. "In Christ and through Christ, [the Christian's] life is linked by a mysterious bond to the lives of all other Christians in the supernatural union of the Mystical Body," so that "the holiness of one benefits others."[16] This truth, confessed in the Creed, encourages us to advance more rapidly along the path of conversion, so that each conversion becomes a true step forward.

Those who asked to receive John's baptism publicly manifested their sorrow and repentance. They submerged themselves in the waters of the Jordan with the desire of being renewed and of giving a new orientation to their conduct; they even asked the Baptist how they should behave in the future. Returning home, however, they found themselves treading the familiar paths of the everyday lives they had briefly set aside in going out to see the Baptist. Here began the real adventure, the struggle to put into practice the good resolutions stirred up in them by John.

It has to be the same with us. The joyous moments of deep faith, the broad panorama glimpsed in realizing the need to change the direction of one's life in order to orient it to Christ, are not the whole story. Everyday like will still presents difficulties, perhaps even serious obstacles. But it is precisely there, in the ordinary events of each day, that the sincerity of conversion must be shown. St. Josemaría said: "To begin is easy; to persevere is sanctity." "Conversion is the matter of a moment. Sanctification is the work of a lifetime."[17]

---

16. *Incarnationis Mysterium,* no. 10.
17. *The Way,* nos. 983 and 285.

To persevere requires effort and specific resolutions, with a holy zeal to rectify a little each day, without surrendering to fatigue or discouragement. This perseverance is not the fruit of our own strength of will. Conversion, like faith, with which it is intimately linked, is a gift from God. And from him also comes the strength to continue striving to change.

The effort to begin, and begin again, must be grounded in prayer: intimate and personal conversation with the Three Divine Persons. Conversion requires docility to the Holy Spirit, who guides us on the path to becoming more and more like Christ. It requires that we grow in the mind of Christ and unite ourselves to his filiation, so that the Father of mercy can see in us the face of his Son. It means trusting in the love of our Father God, showing him not our own merits but those of Jesus. It means trusting in Jesus, who gave his life to rescue us from evil and sin. And it requires that we open ourselves to the Holy Spirit, who never ceases to offer us his light, his strength, and, if circumstances require, his consolation.

The effort to convert brings with it a deep joy. God looks upon us with love (as long as we have a right intention), even when the results of our efforts seem mediocre. The initiative is always on the side of our Heavenly Father, who never tires of coming to meet us and granting us his help. "You and I will surely see, with the light and help of grace, what things must be burned and we will burn them; what things must be uprooted and we will uproot them; what things have to be given up and we will give them up."[18]

In the history of many souls, the first step in returning to their Father's house has come from a meeting with Mary. Here is another reason to invoke our Lady as "cause of our joy." From her was born the Savior of the world. And, as the founder of Opus Dei says, "To Jesus we always go, and to him we always return, through Mary."[19]

---

18. St. Josemaría, *Christ Is Passing By*, no. 66.
19. *The Way*, no. 495.

Sin and Forgiveness

The third chapter of Genesis recounts the fall of our first parents, Adam and Eve, in whom all humanity was already in a sense present. At the beginning of human history our first parents sinned, tempted by a serpent who represents the spirit of evil.

Sacred Scripture's stark account does not point the way to a pessimistic view of either creation or history. The refrain "God saw that it was good" marks the creation narrative, and it highlights the capacity for good that God has given mankind.

Still, this account depicts a primordial event underlying a reality we experience every day: ruptures and divisions, confrontations and struggles between and among human beings, and also within each one, in the struggle between good and evil. St. Paul says he experienced a law in his members "at war with" the law of his mind.[1] Original sin underlines the mysterious and deep solidarity of the whole human race, shedding light on our true situation before God and pointing to the arduous path to the good that all must travel.

---

1. Rom 7:23.

The Dimensions of Sin

The Catechism of the Catholic Church gives us two definitions of sin. It is "an offense against reason, truth, and right conscience." It is also an "offense against God . . . disobedience, a revolt against God."[2]

The second definition is closer to Genesis and leads to the heart of Christian revelation. That our actions can offend God indicates first of all that he loves us, and the truth of God's Love is the central message of Christianity. God is not a creator indifferent to the fate of his creatures, insensible to their concerns and trials. He is a God who loves. Furthermore, he is a "jealous God,"[3] who rejoices in our love and is saddened by its lack.

If, however, the definition of sin as an offense against God is primary, the other definition in the *Catechism*—"an offense against reason, truth, and right conscience"—also has great importance. God makes known to us his will and asks us to fulfill it; and his will for us is our good. The divine law is not an arbitrary, capricious legislator's code. It is the rule of conduct of a God who has revealed himself as Love and who, as we read in Proverbs, "finds his delight"[4] in our joy and happiness. It is the law of our well-being.

Disobeying God and violating the truth of our humanity are, in the end, one and the same. Sin offends against God and damages us. It never leaves the person who sins unchanged. Precisely as an act contrary to what we truly are and what we are called to be, sin deforms the deepest core of our humanity. It disrupts the equilibrium between body and spirit and sows disorder in our faculties—intellect, will, and emotions. The mind, subject to the influence of the passions, finds it hard to attain the light of truth and escape from falsehood. The will encounters difficulty in choosing the good, and is strongly drawn to self-affirmation and pleasure. Affections and desires tend to mirror our egotism.

---

2. *Catechism of the Catholic Church*, nos. 1849, 1850.
3. Ex 20:5; 34:14.
4. Prov 8:31.

We also see the traces of sin in the world around us: ways of acting and attitudes far removed from truth that incite others to sin; unjust and abusive situations that persist even after the acts that gave rise to them have ceased. These can become true "structures of sin," as Pope John Paul II called them in his encyclical *Sollicitudo Rei Socialis*,[5] that cry out for rectification.

History can thus be read as a chronicle of a struggle between good and evil carried on in each generation. Each person's path also involves struggle: to face up to one's own offenses against God and their results. Human nature, received at birth and molded by education, is wounded. Not everything spontaneous or instinctive is necessarily good, nor does everything said to be "natural" express true integrity. Indeed, often it is the expression of a deformed nature.

The ascetical struggle and the effort to acquire mastery over ourselves cannot be shrugged off as the residue of a bygone era, reflecting an overly pessimistic view of human nature. Original sin is a fact, not eliminated by ignoring it. Its wounds are plain to see, though not always admitted by those who imagine man's natural goodness to be corrupted only by social relationships. This notion is basic to ideologies that falsely attribute all evils to structures, to misinformation, or to cultural taboos. But experience teaches, and Christian faith with its doctrine of original sin confirms, that evil has its roots in us, and the fight against evil must be waged first of all within our own hearts.

The moral life inevitably entails struggle. This is a noble battle to restore lost harmony—recover the original balance between intellect, will, the passions. This therefore is a positive struggle to grow in virtue and foster the good within us that sin obscures but does not destroy. But it is also a struggle against sin and the deformity it generates.

---

5. No. 36.

The Love that Conquers Sin

In his encyclical *Dominum et Vivificantem,* John Paul II refers to the Genesis account of original sin. Satan, the Pope writes, led Adam and Eve to sin by distorting the truth about God. The serpent began by insinuating that God is not a loving Father who seeks his creatures' good, but an enemy who envies them their happiness. With incredible wickedness, the devil made God the object of man's suspicion.

This falsification is present in every sin. Someone who sins consciously or unconsciously distorts the truth of God's fatherhood by affirming oneself in opposition to the divine law. He sins because he ceases seeing the divine commandment as an expression of the good and no longer considers it attractive. This distortion of the truth about God necessarily destroys the truth about man. Man sees himself no longer as a son but as an oppressed servant, as someone who must rebel in order to affirm himself.

Not without reason does the Gospel of St. John define the devil as "the father of lies."[6] The tempter leads us to sin by deceiving us with the great falsehood: mistrust in God. In every age and epoch the restoration of filial trust in God is a matter of urgency. God is not a despot or a danger for us, but a Father, and to know this opens the path to trust in him. The One who created us out of love knows better than we do what will make us happy. The divine law is the sure path to happiness even on this earth.

Each human being represents a precious treasure in God's eyes. This is why any evil inflicted on a person offends the Father of infinite love. It is not a matter of indifference to God that man wounds himself, and sometimes (through drugs, violence, or sexual corruption) descends even to sub-human depths. But divine love upholds the great dignity of the human person and therefore the importance of human acts: the immense value each and every action acquires when performed for love, and the grave damage wrought by pride and selfishness.

---

6. Jn 8:44.

But sin does not have the last word. Grace does. Despite original sin and all the subsequent sins that mar human history, grace super-abounds. In Christ we have attained freedom from the power and dominion of sin. God did not merely ignore our offenses. He canceled sin, destroyed it, erased it. God does not desire the death of the sinner, but wants him to change his conduct and live. If we accept the forgiveness he offers us, God divinizes us with his grace. He restores our likeness to him, so that we can know ourselves to be his children.

This pardon and elevation are brought about by Baptism and, afterwards, by the Sacrament of Penance. We should be deeply grateful for the Sacrament of Confession, seeing it as the sacrament of joy. A person who loves God as Father doesn't view Confession as a humiliation, but as an opportunity to present one's true condition before God, who is "rich in mercy."[7]

While Confession looks to the past, the sin committed, above all it points to the present—to God's ever-present fatherly love—and to the future: that new life which begins with God's merciful embrace.

As a deeply interior reality the Sacrament of Confession includes personal recognition of one's sins, contrition, and a resolution to improve. But it also includes exterior realities: acknowledgment to the confessor of one's offenses against God, manifestation of sincere sorrow, and absolution. In Penance as in all sacraments, exterior and interior, visible and invisible, come together in signs that manifest and produce the reality of grace, and in this case God's forgiveness.

Anyone who rejects the mediation of the priest ("I confess to myself," some say; or "I confess directly to God") shows that he has not understood the sacramental mystery of Christianity. Confession to a priest does not separate us from God but unites us with him. By going to the priest, we go to God who instituted the priesthood and the Church herself as a sign of his presence, of his having drawn close to mankind. In every sincere and personal sacramental confession one

---

7. Eph 2:4.

hears Christ's affectionate and comforting words to the paralytic at Capernaum: "Take heart, my son; your sins are forgiven."[8]

In 1972 St. Josemaría made a long trip through Spain and Portugal, during which he spoke to thousands of people. In a number of those meetings, both large and intimate, he spoke about the marvel of God's forgiveness in this sacrament. "We are amazed by the greatness of God the Creator, who has made all things from nothing. We are overwhelmed by the reality of God the Redeemer, who comes to save mankind with such great love that he lets himself be nailed to the Cross, suffering all he could suffer. He could suffer all that he wanted to, and he wanted to suffer a lot because he loves us a lot. . . . And finally we turn our eyes to a God who forgives. And then it's beyond all imagining: a God who forgives! Who forgives more than all the mothers and fathers put together forgive their children. It makes me fall in love, it moves me. I am deeply moved! A God who forgives is a father and a mother a hundred times over, infinite times over."[9]

Personal weakness and the mercy of God constantly interact during a Christian's earthly journey. Sometimes grave sin requires a contrite confession; daily there are smaller faults that, being so petty, can be even more humiliating. If we are honest about our weakness, we will not be surprised by these defects. Instead they will move us regularly to approach the Sacrament of Penance, there to meet our Father God once again, to renew our sorrow, and to redouble our desire to improve. "The Christian life is a continuous beginning again each day. It renews itself over and over," St. Josemaría declared.[10]

The saints were not sinless. They were people like us, with the same or similar inclinations, temptations, and defects. Their life stories were not so different from what our own will be if we trust in God's love. "They fought and won; they fought and lost. And then, repentant, they

---

8. Mt 9:2.

9. *Dos Meses de Catequesis*, vol. II, p. 668.

10. St. Josemaría, *Christ Is Passing By*, no. 114.

returned to the fray."[11] In this life, our defeats are never beyond remedy. From the Cross, Jesus sought and obtained from the Father pardon for everyone. Stumble we may, but with faith we can always begin again at the foot of the Cross and from there set foot once more on the pathway that leads to heaven.

---

11. Ibid., no. 76.

Along the Paths of Prayer

St. Mark in his Gospel describes a surprising miracle that took place in two stages. People brought a blind man to our Lord and asked him to cure him. Jesus touched his eyes with saliva, placed his hands on him, and asked him what he could see. "I see men; but they look like trees, walking," the blind man said. Then Jesus placed his hands on him again and the man fully recovered his sight.[1]

Our situation in some ways is like that of the blind man after Jesus' first actions. We see people through a kind of fog that blurs their image. We have a hazy view of everything, especially God.

The cure of the blind man is a parable of our life. The miracle of our transformation into Christ hasn't been brought to completion. We need our Lord to intervene once again in our life, so that we can know him better and more fully grasp the meaning of existence. We need him now, and we will always need him. The miracle takes place little by little in prayer, and will be complete only when we contemplate God face to face in his glory.

---

1. Cf. Mk 8:22–26.

Why Pray?

Opinion polls have popularized expressions such as "non-practicing believers," "partial identification with the Church," and the like. But those who view the life of faith this way have a deformed image of it—as if Christianity were a set of rules, duties, and self-denials. And then they accuse the Church of clinging obstinately to outmoded customs.

Christianity is not just rules of behavior. The shepherds who went to the cave at Bethlehem did not go there for a rulebook; they went to see the Messiah—and they found a child, Son of God made man, in the arms of Mary with Joseph. Here is the heart of Christianity: God who took on our human nature so that we could share in his life, first here on earth and later fully, in heaven.

Christianity certainly includes norms and guidelines for behavior. Jesus said: "He who has my commandments and keeps them, he it is who loves me."[2] But Christ's words show that it is not the commandments that are central but the love from which they draw their meaning. Love means perceiving the person loved as "another I" and wanting his or her good. It means readiness to fulfill his or her needs and desires— even being ready to give our life, because we value the person we love more than we do ourselves.

This reality that marks all authentic love is found in a special way in Christianity, which has its origin from a God who is infinite and perfect Love. "In this the love of God was made manifest among us, that God sent his only Son into the world, so that we might live through him. In this is love, not that we loved God but that he loved us and sent his Son to be the expiation for our sins."[3]

Hence the importance of prayer. Each day we need to set aside time to store up the words of the Gospel and the events of Christ's life, as well as the history of Israel that prepared the way for him. In the Gospels we find that during his public life our Lord was surrounded

2. Jn 14:21.
3. 1 Jn 4:9–10.

by many different people, sometimes large crowds. On one occasion, a multitude left their homes and occupations for several days in order to listen to him and even forgot to bring food. No doubt they returned to everyday life with vivid memories of Jesus' words. But how long did those memories last? Some may have begun to forget almost at once.

But it was different with Peter, Andrew, John, James, Matthew . . . and others whose names we do not know but who decided to accompany Jesus. We see them remaining with him, listening to his words, sharing his journeys and his rest, talking intimately with him and, when the occasion required it, receiving with humility his rebukes. What they saw and heard penetrated deeply into their hearts. At times, not understanding something, they went to Jesus and asked him to explain. Other times, divinely inspired, they grasped the mystery of the Master's life and mission, as in Peter's confession of faith on the road to Caesarea Philippi. "Blessed are you, Simon Bar-Jonah!" Jesus told him. "For flesh and blood has not revealed this to you, but my Father who is in heaven."[4]

These conversations of the disciples with Jesus show us what prayer is. Christ comes to us to meet us now. In the pages of the Gospel, in the tabernacles of churches, at any moment and place, Jesus is with us, in our hearts, and with the Father sends the Holy Spirit to strengthen our faith, to confirm our hope, to nourish our love.

We can listen to Jesus, relive his steps on earth, open our hearts to him. At times, too, we will turn to those who were close to him on earth and now live with him in heaven—especially Mary and Joseph—asking them to teach us to converse with Christ as they did. Other times we will discover the Father and the Holy Spirit.

Every Christian is invited to follow this path, impelled by grace and guided by the Holy Spirit. I repeat: every Christian. John Paul II insisted in his first encyclical: "The man who wishes to understand himself thoroughly . . . must with his unrest, uncertainty and even his weakness and sinfulness, with his life and death, draw near to Christ.

---

4. Mt 16:17.

He must, so to speak, enter into him with all his own self. . . . If this profound process takes place within him, he then bears fruit not only of adoration of God but also of deep wonder at himself. How precious must man be in the eyes of the Creator, if he 'gained so great a Redeemer' and if God gave his only Son in order that man 'should not perish but have eternal life'. . . . In reality, the name for that deep amazement at man's worth and dignity is the Gospel, that is to say: the Good News. It is also called Christianity."[5]

Once we set out on that path, every moment of our life takes on meaning, even when it is arduous or painful. We are filled with joy, desire to serve, eagerness to transmit faith to others, so that they too can share in the joy of knowing themselves to be loved by God. But this is not so for the person who fails to enter upon the paths of prayer. "If you lose the supernatural meaning of your life," St. Josemaria wrote, "your charity will be philanthropy; your purity, decency; your mortification, stupidity; your discipline, a whip; and all your works, fruitless."[6]

In times of unrest and calm, facing a special need or experiencing a triumph, when prayer is easy and when it requires special effort—in the most diverse circumstances, we should seek trusting conversation with our Father God, intimacy with Christ, and familiarity with the Holy Spirit. For this we can count on the help of our Mother, the Blessed Virgin Mary, and the saints in heaven.

The Ways of Prayer

But how to begin? And since begun, how do we continue on the path?

"Prayer," wrote St. Gregory of Nyssa, "is a conversation or dialogue with God." St. Teresa of Avila defined it as "a friendly conversation, often speaking alone with someone who we know loves us."[7] And St. Josemaría said: "You write: 'To pray is to talk with God. But about

---

5. John Paul II, Enc. *Redemptor hominis*, March 4, 1979, no. 10.

6. *The Way*, 280.

7. St. Teresa, *Life*, 8:5.

what?' About what? About him, about yourself: joys, sorrows, successes and failures, noble ambitions, daily worries, weaknesses! And acts of thanksgiving and petitions: and Love and reparation. In a word: to get to know him and to get to know yourself: 'to get acquainted!' "[8]

The liturgy, in which the mystery of redemption is made present, unites us to the prayer of the Church, praising, giving thanks, asking pardon, and beseeching. Brief vocal prayers such as the Our Father, the Hail Mary or the Memorare, or longer ones such as the Holy Rosary or the Stations of the Cross, offer opportunities to savor key passages from the New Testament and compose our own texts. Even while working or going from one place to another or resting, we can wordlessly raise our minds to God or by addressing to him some aspiration or phrase or word.

It is important to have specific periods of time during the day for dialogue with our Lord. The use of a book or a passage from Scripture or notes jotted down at other moments can be helpful. But we may simply want to open our hearts to God or even to remain silent before the tabernacle or a crucifix or an image of our Lady.

Prayer is a realm of freedom: the freedom of the Holy Spirit, who breathes when and how he wishes; and our own freedom, for, knowing ourselves to be children of God the Father and brothers and sisters of Christ, we can express ourselves with the spontaneity of family members. Hence the great flexibility in the ways of prayer.

Think how Jesus prayed. He goes to the Temple in Jerusalem and to the synagogue, and observes the times and forms of Jewish prayer. Before appointing the twelve apostles, he spends a night in dialogue with his Father. At the hour of his Passion, he withdraws to the Garden of Olives to pray. Before working miracles, he calls upon the Father; and afterward he addresses the Father again in thanksgiving. When the apostles ask him: "Lord, teach us to pray,"[9] he responds with the simple and sublime words of the Our Father.

---

8. *The Way*, no. 91.
9. Lk 11:1.

Jesus addresses God as Father, using the familiar term *Abba*, an expression of affection and tenderness in a Jewish family. Jesus wants us to share in his filiation and to express ourselves in the same way. From him we learn that a simple, sincere, and trusting prayer can rise from our hearts at any hour.

Nothing is less like authentic Christian prayer than prideful verbosity. "When you pray," St. Augustine advises us, *pietate opus est, non verbositate,* "piety is needed, not an abundance of words." Nor does the effectiveness of dialogue with God depend on the beauty of our words but on our filial piety, our sincerity of heart, the simplicity with which we show our Father God our love, our longings, and our needs. Let us not hide our neediness from God. After all, he knows it before we tell him. But he wants us to give voice to it, so that his plans are fulfilled with our cooperation.

Christ taught us that God is our Father who loves each and every one of us and seeks us out with infinite generosity. Even when we distance ourselves from him, he waits for us, to receive us back with a kiss of forgiveness and an embrace of joy. Sometimes, because it is for our good, he puts our faithfulness to the test but he always grants us the grace to overcome every obstacle.

Simplicity, trust, sincerity, spontaneity, perseverance—these are some marks of authentic prayer. And so is its contemplative character. "Contemplative prayer is the simplest expression of the mystery of prayer. It is a gift, a grace; it . . . is a communion in which the Holy Trinity conforms man, the image of God, 'to his likeness.'"[10] The content of our prayer varies according to circumstances, but one element must always be part of it: deep and active faith in God's presence, the conviction that he hears us, the effort to look at him with love and intimacy, knowing that he looks at us.

With God's grace, too, this contemplative attitude should be a constant part of our life, present not only in the times dedicated to prayer

---

10. *Catechism of the Catholic Church,* no. 2713.

but throughout the day—in work, in sorrows, in joys. Then we will realize the ideal St. Josemaría so often proclaimed: that we be "contemplatives in the midst of the world"—*nel bel mezzo della strada*, in the middle of the street, as he liked to say.

A sense of our smallness may prompt us to draw back; but, as the psalm says, God loves us not for our personal value or merit, but *quoniam bonus*, because of his goodness. He knows every corner of our hearts and yearns to draw us to himself.

Authentic prayer always leads to practical resolutions to improve. A prayerful soul naturally asks St. Paul's question: "What shall I do, Lord?"[11] The seal of authentic prayer lies in accepting Christ's invitation to follow him perseveringly come what may. Jesus said, "Not every one who says to me, 'Lord, Lord,' shall enter the kingdom of heaven, but he who does the will of my Father who is in heaven."[12]

Prayer leads one to cry out "my Father" as the expression of a unique encounter: mine, despite my nothingness, because you give yourself to me. And at the same time, "our Father!"—expressing the awareness that the infinite love with which God loves each person embraces all men and women and makes us all brothers and sisters. The source of Christian prayer is not an individualistic desire for perfection but divine love that knows no limits.

---

11. Acts 22:10.
12. Mt 7:21.

CHAPTER

9

The Eucharist and the Theological Virtues

"At the Last Supper, on the night he was betrayed, our Savior instituted the eucharistic sacrifice of his Body and Blood. This he did in order to perpetuate the sacrifice of the Cross throughout the ages until he should come again, and so to entrust to his beloved Spouse, the Church, a memorial of his death and resurrection: a sacrament of love, a sign of unity, a bond of charity, a paschal banquet in which Christ is consumed, the mind is filled with grace, and a pledge of future glory is given to us."[1]

Thus the Second Vatican Council summed up the riches of the Eucharist. It is so sublime that, in a certain sense, it encapsulates all the mysteries of faith: the life of the Trinity, whose love is manifested in the Mass; the Incarnation, for the Eucharist contains Christ's Body and Blood; Redemption, made present in the sacrifice of the altar; the action of the Holy Spirit, fruit of the Cross, in and through whom we share in the banquet of love anticipated in the Eucharist.

---

1. Vatican II, *Sacrosanctum Concilium*, no. 47.

St. John tells us: "Now before the feast of the Passover, when Jesus knew that his hour had come to depart out of this world to the Father, having loved his own who were in the world, he loved them to the end."[2] Anticipating the offering of his life on the Cross, Jesus showed his love as fully as possible by establishing the sacrament of his Body and Blood.

Jesus gives us himself in the Eucharist because he knows that we need him. Before multiplying the loaves and fishes, he looked at the multitude following him and exclaimed: "I have compassion on the crowd, because they have been with me now three days, and have nothing to eat; and I am unwilling to send them away hungry, lest they faint on the way."[3] He understands that our path through life also is long. Besides bodily fatigue, we are beset by many other difficulties and dangers. Left to our own resources, we will not reach the end of the journey safely. And so he remains with us, sustaining us as food for our souls.

The meaning of this sacrament is grounded in love, and only through love can we understand its greatness. What St. Paul affirms of our future glory is applicable also to it: "No eye has seen, nor ear heard, nor the heart of man conceived, what God has prepared for those who love him."[4] The Eucharist is the fruit of a love that knows no limits. To begin to fathom it and draw upon its infinite riches, we must ask God to increase our capacity to love, so that our eyes are opened. As Richard of St. Victor wrote, *amor oculus est et amare videre est*—love is an eye and to love is to see.

Before Jesus in the Blessed Sacrament: Faith, Hope, and Love

Faith, hope, and charity, virtues that make up Christian life, converge upon the Eucharist.

---

2. Jn 13:1.
3. Mt 15:32.
4. 1 Cor 2:9.

Facing the Eucharist: faith. Firm faith is needed to believe with all one's strength that Jesus Christ is really, truly, and substantially present beneath the appearances of bread and wine. When the priest pronounces *in persona Christi,* in the name and person of Christ, the words Jesus spoke at the Last Supper, bread and wine are no longer present. Hidden to the senses but really present are the Body and Blood of Jesus Christ, and with them his Soul and Divinity: his whole Person.

Before the consecrated Species, faith moves us to repeat the apostle Thomas's exclamation before the risen Jesus: "My Lord and my God."[5] I believe, Lord, that you are here. I affirm it, more than if I saw you, more than if I touched you, because your word, in which I trust, is truth itself.

The prophets foretold that God would come to dwell among his own: that he would truly be *Emmanuel,* God with us. The Incarnation accomplished this, with an intimacy and a love that are prolonged in the Eucharist. "Lo, this is our God," proclaimed Isaiah,[6] announcing the Messiah. "This is our God," we can repeat, marveling before Jesus in the Blessed Sacrament.

Knowing that Jesus is really present in every celebration of the Holy Mass, that he waits for us in every tabernacle, that he listens to hear a word of love, of thanksgiving, of affection—and also of expiation for the offenses he receives every day— should make us eager to take part in the Mass, to visit him in the tabernacle, to go to him in our thoughts. We should not haggle over the time spent keeping him company. It is never time lost.

Facing the Eucharist: hope. Jesus, present beneath the appearances of bread and wine, is the foundation of our hope, for here we see how ardently God wants to communicate eternal life to us, and here we are given the daily sustenance we need—"living bread," the "bread of life."[7] Here we receive the *daily bread* for which he told us to ask for in the prayer he taught his disciples.

---

5. Jn 20:28.
6. Is 25:9.
7. Jn 6:48, 51.

Hope, too, because Jesus—the physician of souls and of bodies, our friend and brother—our remedy. The woman with the hemorrhage was cured by touching the edge of his cloak; what, then, may we hope communion with the Body of Christ will accomplish in our souls?

Living the Holy Mass and receiving the Body of Christ in Communion fill us with optimism for this life and with hope for the next. Jesus gave us explicit assurance: "If anyone eats of this bread he will live forever"; "Whoever eats my flesh and drinks my blood, has eternal life and I will raise him up on the last day."[8] The life Jesus communicates to us is his own. It is eternal life, which he already gives us and which will be manifested fully at the end of our journey.

The Eucharist—the Mass and the Sacred Host—ought to be the center of our desires. "Where your treasure is, there is your heart,"[9] said Jesus. Riches accumulated by cleverness and hard work—and perhaps by guile—are for many a magnet drawing them irresistibly. But the Christian has within his grasp treasure infinitely more precious. In the Eucharist Jesus invites us to speak with him trustingly and to make him the true treasure of our heart.

Facing the Eucharist: love. Love for Jesus in the Blessed Sacrament sums up all the affections of our soul, as expressed in the classic prayer of St. Bonaventure: "May I seek you, find you, run to you, attain you, meditate upon you, speak of you . . . may you alone be ever my hope, my entire assistance, my riches, my delight, my pleasure, my joy, my rest and tranquility, my peace, my sweetness, my fragrance, my sweet savor, my food, my refreshment, my refuge, my help, my wisdom, my portion, my possession and my treasure."[10]

Meditating on the love of Christ, we learn to value the particulars of adoration and affection that help us express our gratitude: the rubrics prescribed by the liturgy; genuflections before the tabernacle;

---

8. Jn 6:51, 54.
9. Mt 6:21.
10. St. Bonaventure, Prayer of thanksgiving after Mass.

bell towers seen in the distance that signal Jesus' presence awaiting us in a church. This simple and constant Eucharistic contact with Jesus encourages us to strive to fulfill God's will in everything.

Holy Mass, Center and Root of Christian Life

Faith, hope, and love toward the Eucharist find their principal object in Holy Mass, the memorial of Christ's paschal sacrifice. The Mass is the making present and sacramental offering of the unique, definitive sacrifice of the new Law, the unbloody renewal of Christ's holocaust on the Cross. It is an act of thanksgiving and praise for the Father, and a manifestation of the power and action of the Holy Spirit. The Mass is "a divine action, Trinitarian, not human,"[11] Here, through the mediation of Christ's Humanity, the Trinity incorporates us into divine life.

The Mass is at the same time the offering of the Church, uniting herself to Christ, her Head, and, with him, through him and in him, offering herself to God the Father. The *Catechism of the Catholic Church* says: "In the Eucharist the sacrifice of Christ becomes also the sacrifice of the members of his Body. The lives of the faithful, their praise, sufferings, prayer, and work, are united with those of Christ and with his total offering, and so acquire a new value. Christ's sacrifice present on the altar makes it possible for all generations of Christians to be united with his offering."[12]

The Holy Mass is thus the culmination of the Church's life. The Second Vatican Council declared it to be the "center and root of the whole life of the priest"[13] and indeed of all Christians, who are called to join the priest in offering the holy Holocaust to the Father and to fill their lives with the sentiments it evokes.

Making the Mass the center and root of one's life was central to St. Josemaría's preaching. Thus: "Keep struggling, so that the Holy

---

11. St. Josemaría, *Christ Is Passing By*, no. 86.
12. No. 1368.
13. Vatican II, *Presbyterorum Ordinis*, no. 14.

Sacrifice of the Altar really becomes the center and the root of your interior life, and so your whole day will turn into an act of worship—an extension of the Mass you have attended and a preparation for the next. Your whole day will then be an act of worship that overflows in aspirations, visits to the Blessed Sacrament and the offering up of your professional work and your family life."[14]

When one tries to live like this, the whole day takes on meaning through the Mass and in reference to it. Everything is a preparation for the Mass one will celebrate or attend and also is an act of thanksgiving for the Mass just celebrated or attended. But let us not forget: Jesus is the protagonist—simultaneously priest and victim—of the Holy Sacrifice that is celebrated each day on the altar. He is the one who invites us to the great banquet of Communion as well as the food in which we partake. "We should receive our Lord in the Eucharist as we would prepare to receive the great ones of the earth, or even better: with decorations, with lights, with new clothes. . . . And if you ask me what sort of cleanliness I mean, what decorations and what lights you should bring, I will answer you: cleanliness in each one of your senses, decoration in each of your powers, light in all your soul."[15]

Along with preparing for Mass and participating in it, it also is important to spend a few minutes after Communion giving thanks. This is a time to converse with Jesus Christ, King, Teacher, Physician, Friend—God! It is a moment to manifest our ardent love and our neediness. And this encounter with Jesus should be recalled and renewed throughout the day.

"Do this in memory of me." With these words, which the priest repeats immediately after the Consecration, Jesus instituted the ministerial priesthood. They are directed especially to priests, to whom our Lord gave the mission of perpetuating the sacramental celebration; but they are also addressed to all his disciples, whom our Lord

---

14. St. Josemaría, *The Forge*, no. 69.
15. *The Forge*, no. 834.

wants to draw strength from his death and resurrection and lead a new life in him.

"Do this in memory of me." Jesus seeks souls in love. One to whom this request seemed excessive would understand very little about true, loving friendships. In taking part in the Holy Mass, the faithful draw close to the Holy Cross and identify themselves with the Crucified One; in receiving Communion they are transformed into Christ—"Christified." Now they can say with St. Paul: "It is no longer I who live, but Christ who lives in me."[16]

---

16. Gal 2:20.

CHAPTER

10

Transcending Loneliness

I n the world's great cities millions of people rush about engaged in frenetic activity. There is constant movement and noise. Yet, in this setting people often suffer the bitter sensation of loneliness. Why is this? Why so many old people living alone, children without families or companions, workers isolated in their jobs?

Loneliness is an evil typical of an individualistic culture that sees man as a self-sufficient being with no need of others. The spread of this mentality has weakened interpersonal bonds among relatives, friends, and colleagues. Bit by bit, relationships are replaced by superficial ties of interest or utility.

The Pain and Bitterness of Loneliness

Loneliness is an assault on the needs of our human nature, since a human person is by definition someone open to others. In the first pages of Sacred Scripture the Creator declares: "It is not good that the man should be alone; I will make him a helper fit for him."[1] And

---

1. Gen 2:18.

so from the start we have the fundamental duality of man and woman, the original nucleus of sociability. Before woman's creation, Adam lives in the midst of natural phenomena of animals and plants. But he feels alone, and that feeling is only overcome when someone equal to himself stands beside him. The human person is called to live with others, to share each day's events, both joys and sorrows, with other persons. Only by living alongside others, in family, friendships, work, do we find the full meaning of our own lives.

Why do human beings need social relationships and friendship? Christian faith gives the ultimate explanation: God is not a solitary Being, but a Trinity of Persons—Father, Son, and Holy Spirit—in an eternal and unceasing community of love; and we human beings have been created in the image and likeness of God, called to develop our own "I" in communion with others. Therefore only love—not selfish desire but a love that is benevolent, desiring the good for the other person—draws us out of our loneliness. Simple physical nearness is not enough, nor is superficial conversation, nor a purely technical collaboration in common projects or enterprises. Love in its various forms—conjugal, parental, filial, fraternal, that between friends—is essential to escape loneliness.

But as experience and literature both attest, no matter how successful communication might seem to be, the threat of isolation never completely disappears. It often happens, for example, that love—in itself reciprocal—does not meet with a response or does not attain the desired degree of intensity. Then a shadow of bitterness arises capable of clouding what has already been attained. At other times, interpersonal communication is far from perfect. Others may be sincerely ready to accompany us in painful moments (which mitigates our suffering, and for which we are truly grateful), yet suffering is nontransferable. Each of us dies alone.

"You have made us for yourself, and our hearts are restless till they rest in you."[2] St. Augustine's familiar words hold the key to the problem of the imperfection of human love. Only the Infinite Being, God

---

2. *Confessions*, 1:1.

himself, can satisfy the human capacity for the infinite. Nothing and nobody except God can fill the deep need in our hearts. Thus even the greatest human friendships and human loves contain an element of loneliness. This causes some to close in on themselves so as to preserve a core of intimacy closed against others. Some instead reach out, always seeking something more, in a display of restlessness that can reach genuine repose only in God.

We need to ascend through prayer and love until we reach God, the final dwelling place of our hearts. St. Josemaría wrote: "Consider what is most beautiful and most noble on earth, what pleases the mind and the other faculties, and what delights the flesh and the senses. . . . And the world, and the other worlds that shine in the night: the whole universe. Well this, along with all the follies of the heart satisfied, is worth nothing, is nothing and less than nothing compared . . . with this God of mine!—of yours! Infinite treasure, pearl of great price, humbled, become a slave, reduced to the form of a servant in the stable where he chose to be born, in Joseph's workshop, in his passion and in his ignominious death . . . and in the madness of Love which is the blessed Eucharist."[3]

In the infinity of God's love, each of us is a beloved "thou" before the infinite "Thou" of God. Here our anxieties are quieted, and our inner monologue is replaced by a dialogue with our Father, while loneliness is replaced by the overflowing peace and joy of companionship, including companionship with other people. The encounter with God does not isolate but unites, moving us to love. Knowing the love of God, one desires that all men and women share in that fullness of joy.

Solitude, Recollection, Love

Before beginning his public life and preaching, Jesus withdrew into the desert to spend forty days in prayer and fasting. We also see him at other times drawing apart to an isolated place, guided by the Holy

---

3. *The Way*, no. 432.

Spirit, to be alone with his Father: sometimes, very early in the morning, other times, at dusk or even at night, spending the whole night alone or in the company of a few close friends. Jesus cultivated solitude. His solitude, however, was not a closing in on himself, but an opening wide of his soul, not emptiness but calm recollection.

We all need these moments of solitude, in order to be in touch with the deep recesses of our own spirit and there come to know ourselves and find God. We need to savor being alone with God, falling in love with him and receiving the strength to serve others joyfully. We need to value self-examination, recognizing our faults and seeing the need for the Sacrament of Reconciliation, breaking the circle of isolation and loneliness created by sin, experiencing the sense of God with us that comes with knowing oneself forgiven. These moments of exterior silence, filled with dialogue with God, do not separate us from those around us or from the world; rather, intimate prayer to God deepens love for the world by opening to us the divine reality that lies at its heart.

Christians, as much as anyone else, suffer indifference, desertion, and loneliness. This is the time to recall that Jesus too knew opposition and persecution, loneliness and desertion. Praying in the Garden of Olives, he is alone while the apostles sleep. On Calvary he speaks fearsome and moving words: "My God, my God, why hast thou forsaken me?"[4] At the foot of the Cross his Mother receives in her arms the shattered body of her Son—the moment of her greatest loneliness, when, out of love for all mankind, she gave over to the Father the one she loved more than her own life: her Son.

In the midst of the experience of loneliness, the example of Jesus and of Mary shows us that we are not alone. No matter how great the sensation of abandonment, God is always at our side, sustaining us with his love. The loneliness of a Christian who lives by faith is always an "accompanied loneliness,"[5] loneliness that becomes prayer, petition, union with the Cross of Christ, and so love.

---

4. Mk 15:34.
5. Cf. St. Josemaría. *Friends of God*, no. 180.

Such a Christian will naturally do everything possible to see to it that no one endures the burden of isolation or the coldness of indifference. Recall the events at Naim, where Jesus, seeing a mother's solitude, works a great miracle: the resurrection of her son. In trying to help others who are alone, we must by our words and deeds make known Christ himself. He has promised not to leave us orphans, never to leave us alone, and to accompany us until the consummation of the world. That promise is fulfilled by his gift of the Holy Spirit and by the ineffable wonder of love that is the Eucharist.

Value and Meaning
of the Human Body

"In Christ, God has reconciled the world to himself. . . . In Christ, the world has been redeemed: man has been redeemed, the human body has been redeemed, all of creation has been redeemed." These words are from a 1994 homily John Paul II gave during the inauguration of the restored Sistine Chapel, which the Roman Pontiff described as "a shrine of the theology of the human body."[1] Forming the backdrop were the splendid Renaissance frescoes in which one see united the classical ideal inherited from the Greco-Roman tradition and the Christian ideal, affirming the beauty of creation and the human being and proclaiming God's greatness.

In a homily for Easter Sunday 1967, St. Josemaría said: "It makes me very happy to realize that Christ wanted to be fully a man, with flesh like our own. I am moved when I contemplate how wonderful it is for God to love with a man's heart."[2]

Both quotations agree on a fundamental point: the Christian value of the human body considered in the light of the Incarnation. The Son

---

1. John Paul II, Homily at the inauguration of the restored Sistine Chapel, 1994.
2. *Christ Is Passing By*, no. 107

of God has taken on human flesh in the womb of Mary. He was born in Bethlehem, worked in Nazareth, walked along the roads of Galilee and Judea. And three days after his Sacrifice on the Cross, he rose from the dead, once again taking on his flesh, his body.

The Human Body in the Plan of Creation and Redemption

Shortly after his summons to the See of St. Peter, Pope John Paul II dedicated a number of his weekly catecheses (published later in the book *The Theology of the Body*) to the anthropological and theological meaning of the human body. He took his start from a verse in Genesis: "So God created man in his own image, in the image of God he created him; male and female he created them."[3]

Man is closely linked by his body to the visible, material world. The biblical narrative emphasizes that he was fashioned from "mud of the earth." Yet Genesis does not speak of his similarity to the other creatures, but only of his similarity to God. When Adam, surrounded by a world rich in material beings, sought a creature similar to himself, he saw that he was alone. That solitude, ended by the creation of Eve, showed him that he was not simply a more complex and developed animal, but a being of a different order: it led him to recognize his spiritual dimension, his transcendent personal subjectivity.

The intimate union between bodiliness and subjectivity, between matter and spirit, is the point at which any reflection about our bodily nature should begin. The human body is an integral part, and at the same time an expression, of the person created in the image and likeness of the invisible God. Our bodies manifest what we are and what we feel: sorrows and joys, hopes and fears. Present in the world through the body a human being communicates with others through gestures and words, with tears and laughter. Through the body we influence the

---

3. Gen 1:27.

material reality around us, transforming it from an impersonal environment into "our world," a human world that reflects our personality.

These manifestations express the natural dignity of the human body, which transcends the dignity of the rest of the visible universe— truth obscured both by dualistic and materialistic conceptions of the human person. Dualists, failing to grasp the profound unity of the human being, separate spirit and matter, soul and body, as if they were two different universes merely juxtaposed to each other; materialists, denying the transcendence of the human being, reduce the body to a cog in a material universe with no purpose or meaning. Human beings are the playthings of a blind natural order, and the human body is simply an object or instrument for the attainment of domination or pleasure.

Men and women are, however, far more than mere material objects. We have been created as persons. Nor does our personhood reside only in our souls: human beings are not spirits trapped in their bodies. A human being is a profound unity of soul and body, spirit and matter, forming a single person. No body exists without a soul; and every soul is closely tied to a body, animating and vivifying it and with it constituting a single being.

The human body is realized in two modalities, masculine and feminine, that express the two fundamentals ways of being a human person. This was the Creator's will from the beginning. Some ancient myths to the contrary notwithstanding, the distinction between the sexes did not arise from an original fall or breakup. It expresses God's creative plan, and lies at the foundation of all human society. This is so not only because it makes fruitfulness and procreation possible, but also because it can reflect love in all its forms, provided each person makes a "sincere gift of self" and accepts the other as someone unique and unrepeatable.

In its account of the creation of the human being, Genesis highlights two divine blessings connected with the body: work, the ability to exercise dominion over the natural world and order it to the service of mankind, and procreation, the ability to transmit life and bring new human creatures to birth, which mirrors the image and likeness of God bestowed upon our first parents.

Genesis also sets before us the reality of sin, the primordial disobedience, the refusal by Adam and Eve to accept God's plan. The original harmony was damaged, and God told Adam that the earth henceforth would produce "thorns and thistles" and Eve that the transmission of life would be accompanied by pain. But the blessings were not withdrawn: man and woman continued to bear God's image, and dominion over the earth and ability to communicate life were not taken from them.

God also announced his forgiveness and promised a Redeemer. Prefigured in many ways, this liberation was carried out by Christ Jesus, incarnate Son of God: fully man, with soul and body. He is true God and true man. His humanity, including his bodily being, is a visible manifestation of the mysteries hidden in God. "In his soul as in his body, Christ thus expresses humanly the divine ways of the Trinity,"[4] we read in the *Catechism of the Catholic Church*. "What was visible in his earthly life leads to the invisible mystery of his divine sonship."[5]

This union of divine and the human in Christ Jesus will never be undone. Even in experiencing death, he overcame it; and his human, bodily life, extends into eternity. After his resurrection and ascension into heaven, the eternal Son is present with his body and blood, his soul and divinity, at the Father's right hand: he participates, in his humanity as well as his divinity, in the divine glory and power. My predecessor, Bishop Alvaro del Portillo, spoke of Christ's sacred humanity and of his most Holy Mother as "fully glorified, divinized, the first fruits of what our glory will be like when Christ himself 'will change our lowly body to be like his glorious body' (Phil 3:21)." "But don't forget," he added, "that the divinization of the soul by grace already affects the body to a certain degree."[6]

---

4. *Catechism of the Catholic Church*, no. 470.

5. Ibid., no. 515.

6. Alvaro del Portillo, *Letter of March 19, 1992*, no. 71.

In Christ, each of us is raised to communion with God. The redemption affects not only our spiritual dimension but our whole being. St. Josemaría wrote that even in this life our divinization "affects everything human; it is a sort of foretaste of the final resurrection."[7] And in another place: "Authentic Christianity, which professes the resurrection of all flesh, has always quite logically opposed 'dis-incarnation,' without fear of being judged materialistic. We can, therefore, rightfully speak of a 'Christian materialism', which is boldly opposed to that materialism which is blind to the spirit."[8]

Implications of the Body's Meaning

God wants us to be saints because he loves us infinitely. But sanctity does not only involve the soul. The whole person—matter and spirit—must be sanctified. Sanctity is the fruit of the action of the Holy Spirit, who occupies the whole person in such a way that—as St. Paul says—even the body is converted into his temple.[9] St. Josemaría speaks of "this impressive reality: something as material as my body has been chosen by the Holy Spirit as his dwelling place. . . . I no longer belong to myself . . . my body and soul, my whole being, belongs to God."[10]

What consequences can we draw? Start with one that seems small but is fundamental: respect for the body. I don't mean the inviolable respect for bodily life that someone might try to destroy by mutilating or mistreating the body or injuring health, but respect for the body as such, in its visible reality: in other words, modesty, reserve, a certain "shyness" in regard to the body.

But if God created the body, why this concern about modesty? Pope John Paul II gave quite a profound answer. Prior to original sin, he said, Adam and Eve were naked and felt no shame. But the biblical

---

7. *Christ Is Passing By*, no. 103.
8. *Conversations with Josemaría Escrivá*, no. 115.
9. Cf. 1 Cor 6:19.
10. *Conversations* . . . , no. 121.

text says that after sinning they became aware of their nakedness and covered themselves. As a result of their disobedience, the meaning of their original nakedness changed radically.

But why? The body expresses the person, the human "I." And in doing this it makes communication possible between men and women according to the special communion desired by the Creator: marriage. Physical nakedness is an authentic and true expression of the person if directed to that form of communication, but it loses its meaning to the extent it excludes or hinders it or takes place in a different context.

Sin clouded and disordered the way men and women look at one another; it introduced the possibility of seeking to possess and dominate others rather than giving oneself to them. Thus modesty and reserve became absolutely necessary. Revealing one's own or another's body when that is not necessary (as sometimes it is) is in conflict with human dignity and can lead to one's own corruption or others'. Modesty in relation to others and respect for other people's modesty proclaim and defend the value of the "I," the human person, which should never be treated as an object.

The body also carries our human emotions and passions. These are good in themselves as part of God's creative plan, but they also have been affected by original sin. The Christian worldview joins both dimensions: affirmation of original goodness, and recognition of a wound that diminishes the goodness without destroying it, thus making it harder for us to do what is good. Hence the ever-present need for effort and struggle. In the first place, struggle against the greatest enemies: pride, vanity, ambition, and self-sufficiency, then also in the areas more directly related to our bodily life.

St. Paul wrote to the faithful at Thessalonica: "For this is the will of God, your sanctification: that you abstain from unchastity; that each one of you know how to take a wife for himself in holiness and honor, not in the passion of lust like heathen who do not know God."[11] St. Josemaría said: "We belong to God completely, soul

---

11. 1 Thess 4:3–5.

and body, flesh and bones, all our senses and faculties. Ask him, confidently: Jesus, guard our hearts! Make them big and strong and tender, hearts that are affectionate and refined, overflowing with love for you and ready to serve all mankind."[12]

"Blessed are the pure of heart," says our Lord, "for they shall see God."[13] Purity of heart involves striving to keep one's heart open to a love that ennobles it, and this requires the struggle to prevent our minds and hearts from being sullied by thoughts contrary to human dignity that obstruct communication with others and especially with God. Purity of heart includes chastity but is not limited to it. Christ tells us to guard a purity of soul and body—each in one's own state—that empower one to "see God," by the contemplation of the Creator's image present in all that he creates.

"Some are called to live this purity in marriage," St. Josemaría said. "Others, forgoing all human love, are called to correspond solely and passionately to God's love. Far from being slaves to sensuality, both the married and the unmarried are to be masters of their body and heart in order to give themselves unstintingly to others."[14] That always requires effort, and perhaps especially in a society like ours, with its constant and brazen barrage of sensuality. Yet St. Josemaría insisted: "You know as well as I do that chastity is possible and that it is a great source of joy." As to the source of that possibility, he quoted St. Paul: "*Sufficit tibi gratia mea* (2 Cor 12:9), 'my grace is sufficient for you,' is our Lord's answer."[15]

Chastity, like the other expressions of temperance, implies self-mastery, dominion over oneself, directing one's energies and instincts toward love and service. For this reason one must learn how to say "no" to thoughts and desires in conflict with one's vocation and human dignity.

---

12. *Friends of God*, no. 177.
13. Mt 5:8.
14. *Christ Is Passing By*, no. 5.
15. *Friends of God*, no. 181.

Mortification—self-denial, both spiritual and bodily, interior and exterior—plays an indispensable role. Let no one imagine that "mortification" refers to something obsolete and strange. St. Paul cites a very up-to-date reality to explain it: "Every athlete exercises self-control in all things. They do it to receive a perishable wreath, but we an imperishable."[16]

There is here a great challenge for us Christians. For by our words, and especially our example, we can help others understand the authentic greatness of the human body and, in doing so, themselves find God in the world around them and in their neighbors.

The Blessed Virgin, Mother of God and our Mother, will give us the strength we need. "Do you not know," St. Paul demanded, "that your body is a temple of the Holy Spirit within you, which you have from God? You are not your own."[17] And St. Josemaría commented: "How often, in front of the statue of the Blessed Virgin, Mother of Fair Love, you will reply with a joyful affirmation to the Apostle's question: Yes, we know that this is so and we want, with your powerful help, to live it, O Virgin Mother of God!"[18]

---

16. 1 Cor 9:25.
17. 1 Cor 6:18.
18. *Conversations* . . . , no. 121.

Fatherhood and Motherhood:
A Gift and a Task

When he received his calling from God, the prophet Jeremiah heard these words: "Before I formed you in the womb I knew you, and before you were born I consecrated you."[1] Isaiah similarly expressed deep gratitude to God for having "formed me from the womb to be his servant."[2]

Neither these two great figures nor any of us came into the world by chance. In his infinite love, God knew us and called us one by one from all eternity to a destiny of blessedness. Yet in God's plan human life depends not only on the divine will. We are the offspring of our parents. Conception is the starting point of a new human life and also the end point of a preceding history. As John Paul II said, "the genealogy of the person is inscribed in the very biology of generation."[3]

A Deep Human Crisis

This awareness—that one is a son or daughter—seems to have grown weaker in contemporary society and less decisive in the lives of

1. Jer 1:5.
2. Is 49:5.
3. John Paul II, *Letter to Families*, no. 9.

individuals. The cause may lie in the fact that children are less and less welcome now—indeed, new life is widely rejected.

A key factor in this development is the emphasis placed upon the ideal of the self-sufficient person. In shaping themselves as they like, many people propose to transform the world into a setting for their own gratification. They have no need of anyone else, they owe no one anything, and the fact that they are the offspring of others, far from being a constitutive part of their personality, is only a transitional circumstances to be sloughed off as soon as possible. Childhood is a nuisance; "adult" life is all that counts.

Toward the end of the 1960s "paternalism" became a target of widespread, intemperate criticism. True, "paternalistic" authority, public and private, has sometimes been abused to impose unconditional obedience on those subject to it. But this was not the root of the problem. In the end, the criticism of paternalism was directed against the Christian God, whom Jesus Christ taught us to invoke as *our Father*. Now this God was accused of invading human autonomy.

This way of thinking was a stepchild of deism, which accepted God as creator of the universe but saw him as totally disinterested in the fate of his creatures—an image of God altogether at odds with the God revealed by Jesus as *Abba*, papa. Failure to accept God's fatherhood, "from whom every family in heaven and on earth is named,"[4] inevitably obscures the meaning of human fatherhood, which is reduced to a mere biological function. It also obscures one's own identity, first as a child (owing his or her existence to others) and then as a future parent (capable of transmitting the gift one has received).

In consequence of this, fatherhood and motherhood have lost much of their attraction and perceived value, and society is no longer concerned even to conceal the situation. Demographic decline cannot be explained solely by the indifference of a permissive, hedonistic culture or by Malthusian propaganda. Nor do social, economic, and

---

4. Eph 3:15.

political factors like poverty, unemployment, and the cost of housing account for everything. Rather, the value of fatherhood and motherhood in themselves is now called into question. Having a child is no longer seen as something clearly good and desirable, but only as one option among many: a complex, risky endeavor, whose satisfaction needs to be weighed against its sacrifices. The conclusion, very often, is that it isn't worth the effort.

A Divine Gift to Mankind

Even a sketchy outline like this shows the urgency of rediscovering the great value of fatherhood and motherhood. The Second Vatican Council called procreation "a special participation in [God's] own creative work."[5] It's intention, John Paul II explains, was "to point out that having a child is an event which is deeply human and full of religious meaning, insofar as it involves both the spouses, who form 'one flesh' (Gen 2:24), and God who makes himself present."[6]

God made Adam and Eve sharers in his own power: "And God blessed them, and God said to them, 'Be fruitful and multiply, and fill the earth and subdue it.'"[7] The bestowal of procreative power was a great act of trust on the part of divine wisdom, vulnerable as it was to the moral fragility and evil that mankind has exhibited throughout history. Adam was intelligent and responsible, but he was exposed to many temptations, the worst being to rival and even attempt to supplant his Creator. In recalling the serpent's temptation, one hears an echo of some recent human "conquests"—the *in vitro* fabrication of human embryos, their freezing and storage, their use in experiments, and above all the madness of attempting to clone a human being.

In granting human beings the power of generation, God desires that its use be guided by the same motive that led him to create the

---

5. Vatican II, *Gaudium et Spes*, no. 50.
6. John Paul II, *Evangelium Vitae*, no. 43.
7. Gen 1:28.

world and mankind: love. Love is the desire to seek the good of the other, to give oneself and help others share in the good we possess. It is the gift of self.

Man and Woman's Responsibility

In 1994, in his *Letter to Families*, John Paul II wrote that "*God himself is present in human fatherhood and motherhood* quite differently than he is present in all other instances of begetting 'on earth.'" This is so, he explained, because "God alone is the source of that 'image and likeness' which is proper to the human being, as it was received at Creation. Begetting is the continuation of Creation,"[8] and it is the responsibility of parents—in God's presence—to provide the necessary conditions for it to take place.

Especially since the publication by Pope Paul VI of the encyclical *Humanae Vitae*, the Church has placed great emphasis on this element of responsibility. More than on the biological capacities of the parents, God relies on their spiritual faculties, on their condition as persons, and, therefore, as masters of their own acts. "Responsible parenthood," explains Paul VI in the encyclical just mentioned, "is exercised by those who prudently and generously decide to have more children, and by those who, for serious reasons and with due respect to moral precepts, decide not to have additional children for either a certain or an indefinite period of time."[9]

John Paul II says:

Anyone would certainly read and interpret the Encyclical *Humanae Vitae* erroneously who would see in it only the reduction of "responsible fatherhood and motherhood" to mere "biological rhythm of fertility." The author of the encyclical energetically disapproves of and contradicts any form of reductive interpretation (and in such a

---

8. John Paul II, *Letter to Families*, no. 9.
9. Paul VI, *Humanae Vitae*, no. 10.

"partial" sense), and insistently re-proposes the integral intention. Responsible fatherhood and motherhood, understood integrally, is none other than an important element of all conjugal and family spirituality, that is, of that vocation about which the cited text of *Humanae Vitae* speaks when it states that the married couple must "realize to the full its vocation" (*HV* 25).[10]

In this sense, the Second Vatican Council, in the Constitution *Gaudium et Spes*, affirmed that "special mention should be made of those who after prudent reflection and common decision courageously undertake the proper upbringing of a large number of children."[11]

Keen pastoral intuition moved St. Josemaría to advise married couples not to be "afraid of showing affection for each other. On the contrary, this inclination is at the root of their family life. What our Lord expects from them is that they should respect each other and that they should be loyal to each other; that they should act with refinement, naturalness and modesty. . . . The dignity of their conjugal relations is a result of the love that is expressed in them. And there will be love if those relations are open to fruitfulness, to bringing children into the world."[12]

The vocational call to fatherhood and motherhood is a fundamental part of the path leading to Christian sanctity in marriage. It must be understood in light of an event the Church celebrates on March 25, nine months before the feast of Christ's birth. The solemnity of the Annunciation manifests the Christian conviction that a new human life begins at conception, not birth or any later event.

Mary's decision to say yes to the divine plan was not taken lightly. She grasped the consequences, including the persecution foretold by the prophets. But all that counted for little in the face of the promise of salvation for the human race which that Child would bring about so

---

10. General audience, October 3, 1984, no. 3; in *The Theology of the Body*.
11. *Gaudium et Spes*, no. 50.
12. *Christ Is Passing By*, no. 25.

abundantly. So she accepted motherhood: "Behold, I am the handmaid of the Lord; let it be to me according to your word."[13] And—something she could never have imagined—in accepting her child, Mary became the Mother of God.

---

13. Lk 1:38.

13

Suffering, Illness, and Death

"Whoever does not bear his own cross and come after me, cannot be my disciple."[1] Our Lord indicates here the full self-giving to which he calls his followers. Jesus makes it abundantly clear that Christians must be ready to give their lives as he gave his. This means, in practice, loving the specific circumstances God has designed for one's life, with all the difficulties and hardships they may entail. We must be ready to accept suffering and sickness with a supernatural outlook, and at the end of life, death. Suffering enters everyone's life sooner or later, and each of us must confront it as Christ did, certain of having his help. This is what it means to "take up your cross."

A person's attitude in the face of suffering is an especially clear sign of how he or she is responding to Christ's invitation to follow him. Suffering brings some people closer to God: for they receive it with faith, finding in its burden a call to unite themselves to Christ's redemptive cross. Others are alienated from God: they doubt the goodness of an

---

1. Lk 14:27.

all-powerful God who permits suffering; they may even cite their pain as a reason to deny the existence of the Creator or, stopping short of that, refuse to trust in his fatherly love. Yet the truth is that God does love us, and, although we may not fully understand, he permits these trials as part of the path that will lead us to happiness.

Why Suffering?

To be sure, suffering the death of a loved one, the great tragedies in which we are all participants, do raise disquieting questions. Why? Why now? Why me? Why he or she or they? What meaning does it have? If God loves me, how can he allow such things?

"Sacred Scripture is a great book about suffering," said John Paul II.[2] The Christian message does indeed have an answer to all these questions, although it is incomprehensible to those who look for simple solutions or techniques to immunize themselves against suffering.

Christ did not deny the existence of suffering or promise to make it disappear. Certainly he cured many sick people, alleviated pain and distress, condemned the injustices that lead to much suffering. But he also insisted that we must all "take up our cross." His example on Calvary showed what that means at the deepest level.

With God's help, Christian must work to eliminate or lessen suffering, both their own (not out of selfishness, but so that they can be of more service) and especially others', both those close to us and those far away. At the same time, however, a son or daughter of God, in the depth of his or her soul, must always be ready to accept the trials life brings. Rebellion or rage in the face of suffering would reflect little understanding of Christ's sacrifice on the Cross.

The world was created by a good and benevolent God. Suffering and death entered into history only because of the original sin of our

---

2. Pope John Paul II, Apostolic Letter *Salvifici Dolores*, no. 6.

first parents. In speaking of the first sin, however, Genesis reveals that suffering does not have the final word. God has promised to overcome sin and all that sin has wrought. Scripture sheds abundant light on these matters, culminating in the life and words of Jesus Christ.

Throughout the Old Testament one finds expressed the idea (still current in our Lord's time) that a person's suffering is the result of his own sins or the sins of those closest to him. Regarding the man born blind, the Apostles asked: "Who sinned, this man or his parents, that he was born blind?"[3] The notion of immediate earthly reward for good deeds and immediate earthly punishment for sin supplies an explanation of suffering's cause linked to a narrow idea of justice. It may bring a certain peace of mind. It even encourages us to hope that if we free ourselves or are freed from sin, we shall be freed from suffering, right here and now. And it went hand in hand with another concept found extensively in the wisdom tradition, which saw suffering as a paternal correction helping us to mature while repairing the damage we have done out of carelessness or malice.

Both on the human plane and from the perspective of faith these explanations certainly contain truth. Nevertheless, the logic of direct temporal retribution cannot explain everything that happens to us in this life. Other texts from the Old Testament, especially the book of Job, make that clear. The just man Job, deprived of his goods and overwhelmed by immense sufferings, dialogues with his friends, who attempt to explain his trials as punishment for a grave sin Job must have committed and refuses to acknowledge. God himself gives the lie to these accusations: Job is innocent. Writes John Paul II, "While it is true that suffering has a meaning as punishment, when it is connected with a fault, it is not true that all suffering is a consequence of a fault and has the nature of a punishment."[4]

These considerations, and the biblical texts on which they are based, lead to a broader view that sees suffering as something other

3. Jn 9:2.
4. Pope John Paul II, Apostolic Letter *Salvifici Dolores*, no. 11.

than automatic retribution. Here, however, a new and especially difficult question arises: the suffering of innocent people, which scandalizes some, or at least causes them great difficulty. The book of Job, although it does not offer a clear answer, concludes by saying human beings should not try to know and judge the hidden plans of divine wisdom. Thus it ends by asking for an act of faith, which is beyond purely human reasoning.

Other Old Testament passages highlight the value of the suffering of those chosen by God: Moses, Elias, Hosea, Jeremiah, and many other just men and women whose lamentations comprise part of the prophetic writings and psalms. All culminate in the suffering Servant of Yahweh in the book of the prophet Isaiah: "He has borne our griefs and carried our sorrows; yet we esteemed him stricken, smitten by God, and afflicted. But he was wounded for our transgressions, he was bruised for our iniquities; upon him was the chastisement that made us whole, and with his stripes we are healed."[5] These texts still point to a relationship between suffering and sin, but one quite different from direct retribution. This is the suffering of an innocent person, chosen and loved by a God who heals the guilt of sinners.

There is a likeness between Isaiah's words and the lament of David over the death of his son Absalom. Absalom rebelled, took up arms against David, and forced him to flee. Yet as soon as David heard of Absalom's death, he sobbed: "O my son Absalom, my son, my son Absalom! Would I had died instead of you."[6] These words may simply be David's unburdening of his heart; but in giving voice to love that seeks to suffer in the place of another, they suggest that God, moved by fatherly love, might somehow be ready to give his life for his rebellious children—that is, for us.

What is a hint and foreshadowing in the Old Testament becomes a reality in the New. Christ suffers and dies out of love. The Father sends his Son so that, in giving his life for us as a definitive sign of God's love,

5. Is 53:4–5.
6. 2 Sam 18:33.

86

the Spirit will flow forth from his Cross, bringing us the possibility of faith and salvation. Suffering's mysteriousness remains. But in the context of God's infinite love and compassion, we have reasons for trust. Confronting suffering, sickness, and death, St. Josemaría Escrivá wrote,

A Christian can find only one genuine answer, a definitive answer: Christ on the Cross, a God who suffers and dies, a God who gives us his heart opened by a lance for the love of us all. Our Lord abominates injustice and condemns those who commit it. But he respects the freedom of each individual. He permits injustice to happen because, as a result of original sin, it is part and parcel of the human condition. Yet his heart is full of love for men. Our suffering, our sadness, our anguish, our hunger and thirst for justice. . . . he took all these tortures on himself by means of the cross . . . [For someone facing the undeniable reality of suffering,] the remedy is to look at Christ.[7]

We need to learn the "wisdom of the Cross." Christ's suffering brings us to the heart of the divine plan for salvation: the overcoming of sin through God's infinite love, manifested in his total self-giving. Our Lord's violent death was thus not the Gospel's final word, any more than punishment was the final word in Genesis. Christ's passion and death are closely joined to his resurrection. As we read in St. Luke: "He opened their minds to understand the scriptures. And he said to them, 'Thus it is written, that the Christ should suffer and on the third day rise from the dead.' "[8] The risen Jesus' words remind us that our God is a God of love and of life: he conquers sin and death—which stems from sin, from a lack of love—precisely through his Love, thus allowing us to be reborn into a new life that will never end.

Sharing in the Mystery of Suffering

Christ nailed to the Cross is the path. Uneasiness in the face of suffering will always be part of our experience in this life, perhaps because we

---

7. *Christ Is Passing By,* no. 168.
8. Lk 24:45–46.

cannot fully fathom the abyss of evil opened by sin. But in contemplating the Cross, we understand that God is no stranger to human suffering. He accepted it in Christ and made it his own. Christ sought those sufferings because he wanted to save us. Without suffering, without sacrifice, there is no true love.

"Blessed are they who mourn, for they shall be comforted,"[9] Jesus declared in the Sermon on the Mount. Only in heaven will we attain perfect happiness. But Christ, by his self-giving, has already offered us the consolation of his love. In taking our suffering upon himself, he has given it a new meaning. This radical transformation extends even to our death.

After Christ, suffering is no longer seen as a punishment, but as a path of salvation and divinization. Death is not a descent into Sheol, an abyss where there is only a shadowy life and no one can praise God; rather it is the doorway into the house of the Father, where, accompanied by our brothers and sisters, we rejoice in him forever.

Suffering in all its forms, including the suffering that results from mistakes we later deeply regret, becomes a path to fuller identification with Christ, a way of strengthening our condition as God's sons and daughters, a sign that God accepts us as his children and invites us to share in his redemptive work. "God is my Father, even though he may send me suffering. He loves me tenderly, even while wounding me. Jesus suffers, to fulfill the Will of the Father. . . . And I, who also wish to fulfill the most holy Will of God, following in the footsteps of the Master, can I complain if I too meet suffering as my traveling companion? It will be a sure sign of my sonship, because God is treating me as he treated his own Divine Son."[10] We can say with St. Paul: "Now I rejoice in my sufferings for your sake, and in my flesh I complete what is lacking in Christ's afflictions for the sake of his body, that is, the church."[11]

---

9. Mt 5:4.
10. St. Josemaría, *The Way of the Cross*, First Station.
11. Col 1:24.

The sufferings human beings inflict on one another testify to the great power of evil: injustice, oppression, violence, war, homicide. The path chosen by God to free us from this ocean of iniquity stemming from sin passes through the suffering Christ, voluntarily sought out and accepted, in which his followers freely share. This is not because suffering is a punishment that meets a demand for full satisfaction (that is never God's attitude), but because its voluntary acceptance as a way of erasing sin is an expression of love. "Greater love has no man than this, that a man lay down his life for his friends."[12]

It is also true that "sorrow is the touchstone of Love."[13] Contrition, manifesting the sorrow one feels, destroys guilt. Thus sorrow becomes a love that is purified and purifies.

---

12. Jn 15:13.
13. *The Way*, 439.

The Christian Meaning of Time

There is nothing that does not owe its existence to God the Creator. This is true also of time, a measure not of God's life but of the world that came forth from his hands, where change occurs, birth and death are realities, and life involves both growth and decline. And although human beings to some extent escape the limitations of the temporal (we remember the past and in imagination reach out to the future and even arrange it), nevertheless our ability to transcend time is not absolute. On the contrary, we are subject to time and to change and aging.

Only God, in his infinite perfection, is beyond all measurement by time. He knows neither change nor decay. In God there is only the fullness of eternity.

Yet along with being beyond time—or better, without time—God is present in the flow of human events, in the movement of history and in our lives. God looks at us with fatherly love, revealing himself as one who draws close to human beings, walks beside them, is present in their lives. Human history itself is seen to be a history of salvation.

There are moments of special significance in this history: the making of promises to Noah, the choice of Abraham, the covenant with Israel, the repeated sending of the prophets to the chosen people. "I will make my abode among you," God tells the people of Israel, "and my soul shall not abhor you. And I will walk among you, and will be your God, and you shall be my people."[1]

God's successive interventions in Israel's history announced and prepared for his definitive manifestation in Christ Jesus. This did not come about via mass movements or cosmic convulsions, but with the simplicity of the birth of a child—but a child who is God. In Jesus of Nazareth, the Word of God incarnate, the divine and the human, the temporal and the eternal, are united.

Contemplating this great mystery, the Church sings in one of her Christmas prefaces: "No eye can see his glory as our God, yet now he is seen as one like us. Christ is your Son before all ages, yet now he is born in time. He has come to lift up all created realities to himself, to restore unity to creation."[2]

The birth, life, death, and resurrection of Jesus mark the fullness of time, the culmination of history, the moment standing at the very epicenter of time. Unlike other events in history, this one is always present. For it is a moment lived by the eternal Son of God in whom time participates in eternity. "The whole of human history," says John Paul II, "in fact stands in reference to him: our own time and the future of the world are illumined by his presence. He is 'the Living One' (Rev 1:18), 'who is, who was, and who is to come' (Rev 1:4). Before him every knee must bend, in the heavens, on earth and under the earth, and every tongue proclaim that he is Lord (cf. Phil 2:10–11)."[3]

A new and definitive era begins with Jesus. To recall his birth and life is not so much to celebrate an anniversary as to point to the real possibility—fully relevant today—of mankind's union with God. Time

---

1. Lev 26:11–12.
2. Preface II of Christmas.
3. John Paul II, Bull of Indiction *Incarnationis Mysterium*, no. 1.

following Christ is now "the time of the Church," whom the Church, the new people of God called together by Christ and vivified by the Holy Spirit, travels as a pilgrim on earth to make her Lord known.

After Christ, the years and centuries roll steadily on, but he is never transcended or left behind. "In the spiritual life," the founder of Opus Dei said, "there is no new era to come. Everything is already there, in Christ who died and rose again, who lives and stays with us always. But we have to join him through faith, letting his life show forth in ours to such an extent that each Christian is not simply *alter Christus*: another Christ, but *ipse Christus*: Christ himself!"[4]

Our human time will some day come to an end, for each person as well as for humanity as a whole. Then Jesus' second coming will mark the end of history. This will be the definitive encounter of men with God, the realization of the unity of the human race, the transformation of the cosmos—"a new heaven and a new earth," with no weariness or tears or death.[5]

In the Time of the Church

The time of the Church is, above all, a time for continually proclaiming Christ, conserving his memory and transmitting it to each new generation. All of us in the Church have the mission of proclaiming Jesus Christ. Bishops and priests do that by preaching the word; fathers and mothers when, in the intimacy of the home, they teach their children to pray and transmit a model of Christian behavior; theologians and philosophers by reflecting on divine revelation and relating it to science and culture; teachers and educators by helping to form their students; men and women of the most diverse professions, by the Christian witness of their words and deeds. "Christ is urging us," said St. Josemaría. "Each one of us has to be not only an apostle, but an apostle of apostles,

---

4. *Christ Is Passing By*, no. 104.
5. Cf. 2 Pet 3:13; Rev 21:1, 4.

bringing others along, so that they in turn will encourage others to make Jesus Christ known to everyone." He also explained how this was to be done:

> Naturally, simply, living as you live in the middle of the world, devoted to your professional work and to the care of your family, sharing the noble interests of men, respecting the rightful freedom of every man. . . . If we act in this way, we give those around us the example of a simple and normal life which is consistent, even though it has all the limitations and defects which are part and parcel of the human condition. And when they see that we live the same life as they do, they will ask us: Why are you so happy? How do you manage to overcome selfishness and comfort-seeking? Who has taught you to understand others, to live well and to spend yourself in the service of others? Then we must disclose to them the divine secret of Christian existence. We must speak to them about God, Christ, the Holy Spirit, Mary.[6]

The time of the Church, stretching from Christ's ascension into heaven to his glorious return at the end of history, is also the time of faith and of hope: we welcome the good news and wait with loving eagerness for our definitive meeting with our God. And it is the time of regeneration, of human and divine rebirth. Christ has left his Church the treasure of his word and promised her the assistance of the Spirit of Truth; he has entrust to her the riches of his sacraments—Baptism, Confirmation, the Eucharist, Penance, Holy Orders, Matrimony, and the Anointing of the Sick, "footsteps of the incarnation of the Word,"[7] as St. Josemaría liked to call them—are salvific events, moments when the risen Christ transforms souls with his saving power.

Therefore the time of the Church also is a time in which grace is manifested. Certainly sin still exercises its power. But as St. Paul wrote,

---

6. *Christ Is Passing By*, nos. 147–148.
7. *Conversations*, no. 115.

"where sin increased, grace abounded all the more."[8] Our days are days of struggle: we suffer defeats but, with God's help, we also win victories. Consciousness of our weakness should spur us to rely on prayer, to trust in Christ, in the Holy Spirit, and in the Father, and to begin, or humbly to resume the journey.

Throughout the twenty centuries of the Church's history one finds in every time and place heroic testimonies—some extraordinary, others humble—of fidelity to Jesus Christ and his divine message. John Paul II, spoke of "the *fruits of holiness* which have matured in the life of all those many men and women who in every generation and every period of history have fully welcomed the gift of Redemption."[9] But, he added, the Church "always acknowledges as her own her sinful sons and daughters."[10]

This vision should foster in us both holy pride and sincere humility. The time granted to us is a treasure, an opportunity to carry out the mission given us by God. One's earthly path brings with it exceptional moments—usually few in number—and the common concerns of each day. There is a temptation to divide these moments into good and bad—the ones that suit us and those we find unpleasant or mundane. But St. Josemaría insisted: "There are no bad or inopportune days. All days are good, for serving God. Days become bad only when men spoil them with their lack of faith, their laziness, and their indolence, which turns them away from working with God and for God. . . . Time is a treasure that melts away. It escapes from us, slipping through our fingers like water through the mountain rocks. Tomorrow will soon be another yesterday. Our lives are so very short. Yesterday has gone and today is passing by. But what a great deal can be done for the love of God in this short space of time!"[12]

---

8. Rom 5:20.
9. John Paul II, *Tertio Millennio Adveniente*, no. 32.
10. Ibid., no. 33.
11. *Friends of God*, no. 52.
12. 1 Cor 10:31.

Our time in this life can and should be immersed in the very life of God. God became man to share human temporality and raise it to eternity, and this should make us eager to enter upon each day with new love and dedication. Redeem time, spend it facing God, in the service of others. "So, whether you eat or drink, or whatever you do, do all to the glory of God."[13]

CHAPTER

15

With the Strength of Charity

A group of Sadducees who found it hard to believe in the resurrection of the body presented Jesus with a hypothetical case:
"There were seven brothers; the first took a wife, and when
he died left no children; and the second took her, and died, and the
third likewise; and the seven left no children. Last of all the woman
also died. In the resurrection whose wife will she be? For the seven
had her as wife." So misguided was their way of thinking, that, having
replied to them, Jesus concluded with these emphatic words: "You are
quite wrong."[1]

Shortly afterward he was approached by a scribe encouraged by the
Master's clear reply. This scribe had a very different question: "Which
commandment is the first of all?"[2] The query probably reflected the
complexity in interpretations of the Mosaic law that had proliferated
over the centuries. The scribe seems to have been sincerely concerned
to know the truth. Jesus replied: "The first is, 'Hear, O Israel: The Lord
our God, the Lord is one; and you shall love the Lord your God with

1. Cf. Mk 12:18–27.
2. Mk 12:28.

all your heart, and with all your soul, and with all your mind, and with all your strength.' The second is this, 'You shall love your neighbor as yourself.' There is no other commandment greater than these." And the scribe's sincere acceptance of Christ's teaching makes him deserving of the Master's praise: "You are not far from the kingdom of God."[3]

The New Commandment

This is one of the central affirmations of the Christian message. Jesus points to the commandment of charity as the distinctive mark of his followers. "By this all men will know that you are my disciples, if you have love for one another."[4]

Neither dress nor speech nor attendance at certain ceremonies makes one a Christian, but the attitude of one's heart. As St. Paul so eloquently wrote in his first letter to the Corinthians: "If I have prophetic powers, and understand all mysteries and all knowledge, and if I have all faith, so as to remove mountains, but have not love, I am nothing. If I give away all I have, and if I deliver my body to be burned, but have not love, I gain nothing."[5] And St. Augustine provides this masterful commentary: "Let all sign themselves with the sign of the cross of Christ; let all respond, Amen; let all sing Alleluia; let all be baptized, let all come to church, let all build the walls of churches: The only way to discern the children of God from the children of the devil is by charity. They who have charity are born of God; they who have it not, are not born of God. A mighty token, a mighty distinction! No matter what you have, if this alone you have not, it profits you nothing. If you have not other things, but have this, and you have fulfilled the law."[6]

Look again at that dialogue between Jesus and the man who wanted to know "the first of all the commandments." The scribe

---

3. Cf. Mk 12:28–34.
4. Jn 13:35.
5. 1 Cor 13:2–3.
6. St. Augustine, *Commentary on the First Epistle of St. John*, 5, 7.

asked for just one, but the Master cited two, and, although they are inseparable, assigned them an order of priority as two faces of a single coin.

For those who want to be faithful to Christ, there is no separating love for God and love for neighbor. "If any one says, 'I love God,' and hates his brother, he is a liar; for he who does not love his brother whom he has seen, cannot love God whom he has not seen."[7] What do "see" and "not see" mean here? Obviously, no one can see God with his eyes, whereas the needs and concerns of those around us are generally quite perceptible. But although St. John may well have had this meaning in mind, there is a much richer message: In the people around us we discern the God hidden from our bodily eyes. Our Lord tells us he is present in the person of our neighbor—every man or woman reveals God to us. The two commandments, then, are inseparable. Or better, they form a single commandment. Taken together, and in the order he stated, they sum up the law of Christ.

"By his incarnation, the Son of God has united himself in some fashion with every man."[8] Christ became incarnate for us, shedding his blood on the Cross as a pledge of our salvation. "Christ is in some way united" with every human being, says John Paul II, "even when man is unaware of it."[9] Each person manifests Christ to us.

Consider the Master's description of the last judgment. The just and sinners alike will be surprised by the words the Son of Man speaks from his throne of glory. "Lord, when did we see you hungry or thirsty, homeless or naked, sick or in prison . . . ?" "Truly I tell you that when you did this (or failed to do it) for one of the least of my brethren, you did it (or failed to do it) for me."

Serving others means serving Christ, refusing to help them means refusing to help him. He is present in all who suffer any need: hunger, pain, loneliness and alienation, the absence of direction or meaning.

---

7. 1 Jn 4:20.
8. Vatican II, *Gaudium et Spes*, no. 22.
9. John Paul II, *Redemptor Hominis*.

Jesus is present and needs our help in all of these. We must find him in them all.

Let us turn now to St. John's Last Supper narrative. About to bring his self-giving to its culmination on the Cross, the Redeemer converses movingly with his disciples, opening his heart to them with special intimacy. Twice he presents them with what he himself declares to be a new commandment: "that you love one another; even as I have loved you, that you also love one another."[10] Jesus invites us to love with a love like his own, a love that never ends, knows no limits, does not hold back from giving oneself entirely—love that reflects God's infinite, unfathomable love.

The lesson of Jesus' "new commandment" is that charity requires not only discovering Christ in others but striving to take on Christ's "personality." This is to be *another Christ, Christ himself,* loving and serving our fellow men and women, our brothers and sisters, as he served and loved them.

To see Christ in others and ourselves be Christ for them are complementary duties arising from the marvelous virtue of Christian charity. At times their limitations and defects can make it hard to recognize Jesus in them. And then we may imagine ourselves to be excused, as if the obligation to love them had been lessened or even removed. That is the time to recall Jesus, who forgave the people nailing him to the Cross even as the nails pierced his hands and feet.

Jesus' example tells us that nothing—not others' limitations or their real or apparent mediocrity or the wrongs they commit—excuses us from loving as Christ wants us to love. Doing that, one grows more and more like him, and experiences the joy of intimate unity with him. And because love is contagious—"put love where there is no love and you will find love," said St. John of the Cross—others come to understand charity is the path to happiness.

___

10. Jn 13:34.

Universality of Christian Love

In repeating Jesus' words about the two commandments that sum up the Law, St. Luke adds something that the other evangelists omit. Having heard Jesus' reply, the doctor of the law, "desiring to justify himself," asks another question: "And who is my neighbor?"[11] Jesus answers with a parable.

A man attacked by brigands lies wounded and half-dead by the roadside. Two people pass by, see the wounded man, and continue on their way. Only the third, a Samaritan, shows compassion. He places the wounded man on his donkey, takes him to an inn, and arranges for him to be cared for. Having told this tale, Jesus turns to the doctor of the law and asks: "Which of these three, do you think, proved neighbor to the man who fell among the robbers?" Jesus' story and the tone of his voice have moved his hearer. "The one who showed mercy on him," he replies. "Go," Jesus tells him, "and do likewise."[12]

The love Jesus offered so liberally and wanted those who followed him to have, is truly universal: it knows no limits. Jesus' Heart overflows with the love of God, who "makes his sun rise on the evil and on the good, and sends rain on the just and on the unjust."[13] It embraces all creation, both the small and the great, what is near and what is far— and whenever the need arises, it is shown in deeds. It comes from God, who during his years on earth showed himself deeply human, and so it is expressed with the human affection that always accompanies authentic charity. So, too, with us: "We do not have one heart to love God with and another with which to love men. This poor heart of ours, made of flesh, loves with an affection which is human and which, if it is united to Christ's love, is also supernatural."[14]

Here let us consider two of the dangers that menace love and its universality: exclusive concentration on one's immediate circle, to

---

11. Lk 10:29.
12. Lk 10:36–37.
13. Mt 5:45.
14. *Friends of God*, no. 229.

the neglect of anyone else, and adopting a kind of abstract universality that loses sight of the concrete. A Christian needs a big heart that reacts promptly to others' needs and reaches out to the complex problems affecting the whole of society, even though their solution may be someone else's responsibility and not our own. "While Christians enjoy the fullest freedom in finding and applying various solutions to these problems," St. Josemaría said, "they should be united in having one and the same desire to serve mankind. Otherwise their Christianity will not be the word and life of Jesus; it will be a fraud, a deception of God and man."[15]

There is a danger of remaining indifferent in the face of the great social problems or responding superficially, on the emotional level, without practical consequences. But there also is a danger of concentrating on these big issues, while ignoring or even mistreating—though perhaps not deliberately—those who live beside us. Christian charity does not consist in loving humanity "in the abstract"; the people around us need to be loved "one by one."

Inseparable from the greatest expression of Christ's love—his self-giving on the Cross for the redemption of all mankind—is his infinite affection for each man and woman he encountered on his path: his compassion for the widow at Naim, who had just lost her son, his tears for the death of his friend Lazarus, his words and manner, able to prompt decisions to follow him, as with those two disciples of the Baptist, his warmth and affection even when exhausted. Think of his encounter with the Samaritan woman. Worn out from his travels, Jesus is seated by the well. "There came a woman of Samaria to draw water. Jesus said to her, 'Give me a drink.' "[16] Forgetting his fatigue and thirst, he initiated a conversation that led the woman to a profound conversion and to the decision to bring others to Jesus.

That should be the model for our charity toward each person who passes our way. There is always time to give some help, offer the

---

15. *Christ Is Passing By*, no. 167.
16. Jn 4:7.

encouragement of a smile, a friendly word, good example, to do the other a hidden and silent service or at least offer a prayer. Specific and direct charity like this is the best sign of authentic love. To love neighbors means, above all, desiring and seeking their good. In what does that consist? No two people are entirely alike, but for everyone, in every circumstance, the fundamental and definitive good is God.

If we truly desire the good for others, we will seek to bring them closer to God by making Christ known to them and, in Christ, God the Father and God the Holy Spirit. This means opening up to them by example and word the path to a deep friendship with God. We will speak to them about our Lady, who helps us along the way. We will offer them guidance so that they can walk securely on the path of Christian life. And, with the help of God's grace, we will when necessary show them the path to conversion and remind them tactfully of God's loving demands.

Speaking to the woman accused of adultery, Jesus offered her the balm of mercy and forgiveness. But then he tells her: "Go, and do not sin again."[17] St. Augustine comments that Christ "loved us even though we were wicked, but he did not call us to iniquity. He loved us even though we were sick, but he came to cure us."[18] Jesus corrects us, while also encouraging us. In charity, we too must be ready to exhort our brothers or sisters to set out upon, or return to, the path marked out by God.

Medieval theologians called charity the "form" of all the virtues, directing them from within toward the goal that perfects our humanity: love for God and neighbor. Earlier, St. Paul wrote: "Love is patient and kind; love is not jealous or boastful; it is not arrogant or rude. Love does not insist on its own way; it is not irritable or resentful; it does not rejoice at wrong, but rejoices in the right. Love bears all things, believes all things, hopes all things, endures all things."[19] The love Jesus asks of us may at first seem far beyond our strength. And so it is.

---

17. Jn 8:11.

18. St. Augustine, *Commentary on the First Epistle of St. John*, 7, 7.

19. 1 Cor 13:4–7.

But we can count on God's omnipotent strength—on the Love of God present in us. "God's love has been poured into our hearts through the Holy Spirit which has been given to us."[20] Inviting us to love as he loves, Jesus gives us the ability to do that. In union with God the Father, he sends us the Spirit and, with him, the power to love with God's own Love.

---

20. Rom 5:5.

Sanctification of Work

"All the faithful, whatever their condition or state, are called by the Lord, each in his own way, to that perfect holiness whereby the Father himself is perfect."[1] This teaching of the Second Vatican Council is immensely important for the Church's mission and for every Christian's life. Pope Paul VI called it "the most characteristic element of the Council's teaching and, in some sense, its final goal."[2]

As early as the 1930s, St. Josemaría Escrivá wrote: "You have an obligation to sanctify yourself. Yes, you too. Who thinks this is the exclusive concern of priests and religious? To everyone, without exception, our Lord said: 'Be perfect as my Heavenly Father is perfect.'"[3] All are called to follow Christ and grow constantly in holiness.

St. Josemaría invited people to draw close to God in the midst of the professional, family, and social occupations that form the framework of a Christian's life, and especially the lives of lay people. The

---

1. Vatican II, *Lumen Gentium*, no. 11.

2. Pope Paul VI, *Sanctitatis Clarior*, March 19, 1969.

3. *The Way*, no. 291.

Second Vatican Council, in the Constitution *Lumen Gentium*, similarly announced the universal call to sanctity and apostolate in the varied circumstances of daily life. It stressed that this takes place, as the Latin text says, *per illa omnia*, precisely *through* all these human realities.[4] Christians are to seek sanctity not "independently of" or "in spite of" being in the world, but precisely by taking advantage of being there. Indeed, the Incarnation itself shows us that responding to God's call to be perfect does not require abdicating what is human. The eternal Son of God embraced all noble human realities and gave them their fullest meaning. With the help of grace, Christians should discover the divine meaning of human activities, and make it known to others. Lay people do this especially in their daily work.

The Gospel's Good News about Work

In the first chapters of Genesis God confers dominion over material creation on mankind. In his encyclical *Laborem Exercens*, John Paul II calls this the "first gospel of work." It is developed and reaches its fullness, he adds, in Christ. "For Jesus not only proclaimed but first and foremost fulfilled by his deeds the 'gospel,' the word of eternal Wisdom, that had been entrusted to him. Therefore this was also 'the gospel of work,' because he who proclaimed it was himself a man of work, a craftsman like Joseph of Nazareth."[5]

All the years our Lord spent among us have redemptive meaning. This includes the first three decades of his life, which the gospels scarcely mention. In that silence, however, we see a sign that Jesus' manner of living was completely normal, like that of any other Jewish boy or young man of his time. St. Josemaría drew important insights from this. Jesus, he says, "lived in obscurity, but, for us, that period is full of light. It illuminates our days and fills them with meaning, for we are ordinary Christians who lead an ordinary life, just like millions of

---

4. Vatican II, *Lumen Gentium*, no. 41.
5. John Paul II, *Laborem Exercens*, no. 26.

other people all over the world. That was the way Jesus lived for thirty years. . . . And he was God; he was achieving the redemption of mankind and 'drawing all things to himself' (Jn 12:32)."[6]

Nothing authentically human is foreign to the divine plan of redemption. God is concerned with all the circumstances of our daily life. God has not only brought us into being but given us our capacity to dominate the earth, to perfect it by our work. He seeks our collaboration even in what is most divine, his own work of salvation and redemption.

"By their very vocation," as the Dogmatic Constitution *Lumen Gentium* stresses, the laity are called to "seek the kingdom of God by engaging in temporal affairs and directing them according to God's will."[7] This they do through their daily life and duties in the middle of the world, especially professional work. Work thus acquires a deep supernatural meaning, becoming a participation in God's creative and redemptive work, a sacrifice of praise offered daily to God the Father, with Christ, through the grace of the Holy Spirit.

Lay people are not second-class Christians, and their professional vocation is an integral part of God's plan. By their dedication to their daily work and human relationships, they render service to God and all mankind.

Constructing the World, Cooperating with God

Human progress is good in itself and accords with God's plan. But human beings are capable not only of generous acts of service but self-seeking and pride. The advances achieved by human effort can become pretexts for self-satisfaction, vehicles of ambition, and pride.

God does not ask Christians to renounce their capacity to help build up society and culture. But he wants them to take up their work

---

6. *Christ Is Passing By*, no. 14.

7. Vatican II, *Lumen Gentium*, no. 31.

with a clear awareness of their origin in him and their orientation to him, and to carry it out with prayer, humility, a desire to serve, and optimism. In his homily on May 17, 1992, for the beatification of Josemaría Escrivá, Pope John Paul II said: "In a society in which an unbridled craving for material things turns them into idols and a cause of separation from God, the new *Beatus* reminds us that these same realities, creatures of God and of human industry, if used correctly for the glory of the Creator and the service of one's brothers and sisters, can be a way for men and women to meet Christ."[8]

This is the ideal St. Josemaría had in mind in speaking of the "sanctification of work." Here I shall focus on two points: the importance of personal witness and the redemptive value of human activity.

Our Lord sends us forth as his instruments to make him present in every sector of the world. Right where we are, where our life and work place us, is where Christ and the Church need each of us to make him present.

Called to sanctify themselves in the middle of the world and give witness to Christ among their peers, the ordinary faithful will therefore refuse to look upon work—much less the worker—as a mere factor in production or an instrument for acquiring wealth or attaining prestige or power. They will defend their own dignity and that of everyone else. They will fight fraud and injustice and try always to see those around them as neighbors, and not objects or servants.

A person with faith doesn't act in order to be admired. We Christians have to strive to make Christ's spirit known through our work and behavior, through all our actions. Being a witness to Christ—and every Christian, I insist, is called to this mission—is a title of honor, but also a demanding one.

As to the second point mentioned above: working with a supernatural and apostolic outlook confers on work the value of a sacrifice offered to God. From this perspective consider the great importance for a Christian of unity of life. Christian life does not consist of certain

---

8. John Paul II, Homily at the beatification of Josemaría Escrivá, May 17, 1992.

practices of piety standing apart from work and family duties. Each daily activity should be done with full consciousness of its value in God's eyes—and therefore as well as possible.

To offer sacrifice is a priestly act. All Christians can perform this priestly act because they have received the common priesthood of the faithful in baptism. While differing essentially from the ministerial priesthood, the baptismal priesthood truly participates in the priesthood of Christ, and, united to the holocaust of Jesus Christ, makes one's own life and work a living sacrifice pleasing to God and giving him glory. Joined with Christ by grace, a Christian can address God daily with words the priest says during Holy Mass at the preparation of the gifts, including within them all his or her daily occupations: *sic fiat sacrificium nostrum in conspectu tuo hodie, ut placeat tibi, Domine Deus*— "Lord God, we ask you to receive us and be pleased with the sacrifice we offer you."

The deep redemptive dimension of human work enriches one's professional responsibilities with new meaning. Clearly Christ does not include in his self-giving to the Father work that is not humanly upright, not filled with charity, or that is careless and half-done. So how should we respond to the challenge to make our daily work a sacrifice pleasing to God?

Here is St. Josemaría's answer: "It is no good offering to God something that is less perfect than our poor human limitations permit. The work that we offer must be without blemish and it must be done as carefully as possible, even in its smallest details, for God will not accept shoddy workmanship. 'Thou shalt not offer anything that is faulty,' Holy Scripture warns us, 'because it would not be worthy of him (Lev 22:20).' For that reason, the work of each one of us, the activities that take up our time and energy, must be an offering worthy of our Creator. It must be *operatio Dei*, a work of God that is done for God: in short, a task that is complete and faultless."[9]

---

9. *Friends of God*, no. 55.

For those who realize that they are God's children and share in Christ's priesthood, working well is not just a matter of technique. It is an integrally human act, closely tied to moral good and the service of mankind. Only work like this resembles Christ's work and is worthy of being offered to God as an acceptable sacrifice.

"Add a supernatural motive to your ordinary work and you will have sanctified it,"[10] says a point in *The Way*. So simple . . . and so demanding. A "supernatural motive" is not mere words. It has a decisive impact on the way we work, moving us to work well, in God's presence, with the intention of imitating Christ and serving others. What a great blessing it would be for the Church and the world if all Christians worked like that!

---

10. No. 359.

CHAPTER

17

Detachment, Self-Dominion, Generosity

The Son of God entered our world in poverty, in a stable for animals. Two exalted creatures, Mary and Joseph, gave him love and affection, but they could not give him material goods. There is a profound lesson here about Christian life understood as a pathway of progressive identification with Jesus.

Christ dwells in the soul of each baptized person. As St. Paul tells the Galatians, God has "sent the Spirit of his Son into our hearts crying: '*Abba! Pater!*' "[1] We are children of God in Christ, and the life of the Son must be reproduced in us. An essential element of this process concerns our attitude toward the goods of this earth, which should be one of true detachment, poverty of spirit, a radical and trusting abandonment into the hands of our Father God.

Poverty as a Situation and as a Blessing

What is the Christian message about poverty? Let us look briefly at what the Holy Scriptures say.

---

1. Gal 4:6.

110

The Old Testament shows poverty's twofold significance for the people of Israel. Disadvantaged from a human perspective, the poor nevertheless were also privileged inasmuch as God was concerned about them. All the same, poverty was a hard and unfortunate reality calling for the generous response of the entire community.

The prophets stressed that power and riches could make one attached to perishable goods and forgetful of God. They condemned the abuse of authority, the exploitation of widows and orphans, fraud and violence. They proclaimed that God's love embraced the destitute and that the Messianic goods were promised to them as well. As one of the signs of his coming, Isaiah said, the Messiah would preach "the good news to the poor."[2]

The prophetic writings and many of the psalms extol the deep spiritual meaning of poverty. In this context the poor are not so much those who lack material goods (but this is not excluded and to some extent is presupposed); they are the humble, those upright and just, who suffer yet trust in God despite misery, destitution, and trials. Even more radically, the poor are those men and women of faith who recognize their unworthiness and sinfulness, and feel the constant need for God's forgiveness. Poverty is no longer seen simply as a hard fact. Poverty and human misery of any kind are transformed into opportunities to comprehend one's existential situation of need and reach out to God. "I sought the Lord, and he answered me, and delivered me from all my fears. . . . This poor man cried, and the Lord heard him, and saved him out of all his troubles."[3]

The Son of God assumed the human condition in its entirety, except for sin. He knew heat and cold, hunger and thirst, pain and abandonment, want and poverty. It was not just the poverty at Bethlehem at the beginning; it was also the supreme and solemn moment when, nailed to the Cross, after pronouncing the prophetic words of

2. Is 61:1.
3. Is 34:4, 6.

the psalm—"My God, my God, why have you abandoned me?"[4]—
and identifying himself with the most forsaken of the poor, Jesus
showed his complete and unwavering trust in the Father: "Father, into
thy hands I commit my spirit!"[5]

All through life, from birth to death, Jesus' constant attitude was
one of detachment and self-giving. He did not reject material goods
and his friends included some who were fairly well off, such as Martha,
Mary, and Lazarus. Indeed, for thirty years he lived in his own home,
the simple home at Nazareth, and there with Joseph worked at a trade
like that of others. Even in his three years of preaching he wore a good
tunic, elegant and seamless. But we also see him prepared to renounce
everything, leading a life that was extremely simple, to the point that
he could say: "Foxes have holes, and birds of the air have nests; but the
Son of man has nowhere to lay his head."[6]

Jesus' poverty challenges us precisely because it is voluntary. God
freely chose to become incarnate, and, having done that, he freely chose
the path of poverty for himself. His was not the way of power or riches
but that of love, expressed in detachment and self-surrender. St. Paul
wrote of Jesus that "though he was in the form of God, he did not count
equality with God a thing to be grasped, but emptied himself, taking
the form of a servant."[7] And to the Christians at Corinth: "though he
was rich, yet for your sake he became poor, so that by his poverty you
might become rich."[8]

There is a close connection between poverty of spirit and love,
between detachment from self and the capacity to love. Jesus expressed
this clearly in his words and his life. Consider the Sermon on the
Mount, particularly the beatitudes, where the smallness of human aspirations are contrasted with the greatness of what God offers. "Blessed

---

4. Ps 22:2.
5. Lk 23:46.
6. Mt 8:20.
7. Phil 2:6–7.
8. 2 Cor 8:9.

are the poor in spirit, for theirs is the Kingdom of Heaven."[9] Someone who closes himself up in ambition, in the quest for power or riches, who trusts in his own strength or possessions, diminishes—and may completely lose—his capacity to love; but a man detached from himself and created goods opens his heart to receive the kingdom of heaven.

Jesus leaves no doubt that serving God and being enslaved to material goods are incompatible: "You cannot serve God and mammon."[10] We must abandon ourselves to divine providence and place our trust in God. This is the path that leads to the freedom to love. "And which of you by being anxious can add one cubit to his span of life? And why are you anxious about clothing? Consider the lilies of the field, how they grow; they neither toil nor spin; yet I tell you, even Solomon in all his glory was not arrayed like one of these. But if God so clothes the grass of the field, which today is alive and tomorrow is thrown into the oven, will he not much more clothe you, O men of little faith?"[11]

Poverty of spirit is the way to true joy. Avarice, the search for security in transitory goods, is the path to unhappiness. The "rich young man" of the Gospel believed that he was fulfilling the law. But when Jesus sought to raise his vision to a higher plane then the observance of rules—to the renunciation of material goods—"he went away sorrowful; for he had great possessions."

To his disciples, Jesus comments: "Truly, I say to you, it will be hard for a rich man to enter the kingdom of heaven." The disciples are astonished at the radical nature of the Master's demands: "Who then can be saved?" Christ does not lessen his demand—the self-giving of those who would follow him must be total—but he reminds them they can rely on God's help: "With men this is impossible, but with God all things are possible."[12] And when Peter—perhaps still a bit worried by

---

9. Mt 5:3.
10. Mt 6:24.
11. Mt 6:27–30.
12. Mt 19:22–26.

the drift of the conversation—points out that he and the other disciples had abandoned everything to follow him, Jesus replies: "Every one who has left houses or brothers or sisters or father or mother or children or lands, for my name's sake, will receive a hundredfold, and inherit eternal life."[13]

God asks for everything; he demands a free heart, without attachments or excuses. But he always gives much more. "God does not allow himself to be outdone in generosity,"[14] St. Josemaría said.

Detachment and Generosity

When referring to material possessions, St. Josemaría often used the word "*señorio*"[15] ("dominion"), meaning ease in making decisions, freedom, absence of attachments and enslavements. As St. Paul said: "I know how to be abased, and I know how to abound; in any and all circumstances I have learned the secret of facing plenty and hunger, abundance and want. I can do all things in him who strengthens me."[16] This is what the attitude of a Christian should be: anchoring in Christ and accepting from him and in him whatever life brings. "You will be truly rich when you don't need anything,"[17] St. Augustine remarked.

This detachment is not vague and theoretical. It must have practical consequences. Two stand out: the temperance of an austere life, self-control by which to avoid whims and superfluous comforts; and generosity arising from realization that the material goods God gives one are not for oneself alone but for the service of others.

The Acts of the Apostles says this of the first Christian community: "And all who believed were together and had all things in common; and they sold their possessions and goods and distributed

---

13. Mt 19:29.
14. *Christ Is Passing By*, no. 40.
15. Cf., for example, *Christ Is Passing By*, no. 37, and *Friends of God*, no. 122.
16. Phil 4:12–13.
17. St. Augustine, *Sermon 77*, no. 13.

them to all, as any had need."[18] The seven deacons (literally, "servants") were entrusted with service to the poor. St. Paul organized collections by which Christian communities could help one another.

Christian practice has always included almsgiving. The alms should come not only from superfluous goods, but also from those that are "necessary": giving them up requires reducing one's own standard of living to some degree. The history of the Church tells of countless men and women who have followed the example of those early Christians: both individuals and institutions, ranging from religious orders and congregations to more recent volunteer groups who care for the poor, refugees, victims of natural disasters, addicts, the infirm or old people living alone. . . . Indifference to others' needs would be a sign of diminished Christian spirit.

From the first centuries, the Fathers of the Church emphasized that those who possess material resources are stewards. They have received their possessions in trust from God, to provide a service to the community. The Second Vatican Council repeated this teaching: "God destined the earth and all it contains for all men and all peoples, so that all created things would be shared fairly by all mankind under the guidance of justice tempered by charity. No matter what the structures of property are in different peoples, according to various and changing circumstances and adapted to their lawful institutions, we must never lose sight of this universal destination of earthly goods. In his use of things man should regard the external goods he legitimately owns not merely as exclusive to himself but common to others also, in the sense that they can benefit others as well as himself."[19]

Among the great challenges facing society today is the just distribution and correct use of natural resources, within each country and also internationally. The spirit of Christian poverty should move those responsible for the economy "businessmen and government officials, financiers and union leaders" to be exemplary in this matter. Resources

---

18. Acts 2:44–45.

19. *Gaudium et Spes*, no. 69.

should be used for the benefit of all and passed on to future generations with the increase that present efforts have produced.

Urging the Corinthian Christians to take up a collection to help their needy brethren, St. Paul writes: "I say this not by way of command, but to test the genuineness of your love by your concern for others."[20] Here is the impetus of Christian action: love. The Christian spirit of poverty goes far beyond external gestures and simple sentiments of solidarity. It expands the horizons of our intellects and hearts empowering us to make God's will our own and to express love with deeds.

In much the same way, the experience of material poverty is transformed into a school of Christian detachment. Accepted with faith and love, poverty is capable of activating a capacity for the infinite in the human heart. The poor person—poor in whatever sense—who trusts in the Lord, is a visible sign of God's presence. Christians, especially the saints, have always understood this. While doing everything in their power to relieve poverty and suffering, they raise up those who suffer in their prayers.

St. Josemaría often said that in the early years of his apostolate, struggling to launch the project God had shown him, he sought strength among the poor and the sick in Madrid's downtrodden neighborhoods and in hospitals. He devoted hours every day to the priestly work of visiting them and trying to help them. From him I heard repeatedly strong exhortations to be generous in caring for the poor and the sick and to learn from them.

Detachment, generosity, concern for the needs of others shown in deeds, are not impossible ideals. They are within reach by people who open their hearts to God's help. And today, when the persistence of mankind's problems causes some people to be skeptical about the prospects for ever solving them, Christ's example and the grace of the Holy Spirit are sources of the strength we need to turn latent love and generosity into efficacious deeds.

---

20. 2 Cor 8:8.

The Vocation of Christians in Society

"Render therefore to Caesar the things that are Caesar's, and to God the things that are God's."[1] Jesus' words are a fundamental reference point in the efforts of Christians to determine the relationship between their dignity as God's children, called to eternal life, and their condition as citizens of temporal society, members of a great variety of peoples, nations, and political communities.

"To Caesar the taxes, to God your very selves,"[2] St. Augustine says. And he adds: "As Caesar seeks his image on the coin, so God seeks his on man."[3] We are "coins of God," persons created in God's image, and we cannot allow any human power to gain possession of this "coin" with its divine likeness. Even as we fulfill our civic duties, we belong to God.

While warning against absolutist tendencies in temporal society and political totalitarianism, Jesus notes that Christians, like other

---

1. Mt 22:21.
2. St. Augustine, *Commentary on the Gospel of St. John,* 40, 9.
3. Ibid., 41, 2.

men and women, have duties toward the society of which they are part: "taxes to whom taxes are due, revenue to whom revenue is due, respect to whom respect is due, honor to whom honor is due,"[4] as St. Paul puts it.

"Christians," says the *Epistle to Diognetus*, "are distinguished from other men neither by country, nor language, nor the customs they observe. For they neither inhabit cities of their own, nor employ a peculiar form of speech, nor lead a life marked out by any singularity. . . . But, inhabiting Greek as well as barbarian cities, according as the lot of each of them has determined, and following the customs of the local people in respect to clothing, food, and the rest of their ordinary conduct, they display to all their wonderful and striking form of life."[5] It is precisely faith, St. Josemaría stressed, that moves Christians "to play our full part in the changing situations and in the problems of human history."[6]

The Virtue of Justice

Justice is a virtue that fosters a sound structuring of society in keeping with human dignity. In the formulation of the Roman jurist Ulpian, it is "the constant and perpetual will to render to each what is his due."

The Church's social doctrine, grounded as it is upon Revelation and her own experience, contains a great variety of principles and criteria: preferential love for the poor, which involves helping them attain a standard of living in keeping with human dignity; the fulfillment of obligations assumed in agreements and contracts; protection of the fundamental rights of human dignity; just use of personal goods so that they redound to the common good as well as one's own benefit; the payment of taxes; truthfulness in conversations and judicial proceedings; doing work with competence and a spirit of service; respect for freedom of consciences; opening up education and culture to all men

---

4. Rom 13:7.
5. *Epistle to Diognetus*, V, 1–4.
6. *Christ Is Passing By*, no. 99.

and women; attention to the handicapped and those who lack opportunities others have; and much else.

Violations of justice are similarly numerous: unjust appropriation
of others' goods; salaries that fail to meet the needs of workers and their
families; discrimination against women in employment; administrative
and business corruption; excessive profit-seeking; inadequate housing
that almost compels families to limit the number of children; exploitation practices in the employment of immigrants; racist or xenophobic
attitudes; technological degradation of the environment; and so on.

Justice is pervaded by the dynamism of another, higher virtue:
charity, love. The Founder of Opus Dei underlined the fact that issues
in the interactions between persons are never solved "simply by addi-
tion and subtraction. . . . When justice alone is done, don't be surprised if people are hurt. . . . Our motive in everything we do should
be the Love of God, which makes it easier for us to love our neighbor
and which purifies and raises all earthly loves to a higher level."[7]

Charity is a sham unless it is based on justice. At the same time,
however, the exercise of love in disinterested service of others com-
pletes and transcends justice.

Politics and its Implications

The relationships governed by justice have a social dimension usually called "political life" or simply "politics." In some sectors, politics has become a derogatory term, as though inherently tainted by
self-seeking, treachery, and intrigue. Occasionally, it even is said that
Catholics should not take part in politics or, if they do, should first set
aside their principles and beliefs, since otherwise they would fall into
fundamentalism.

Politics in itself is a noble activity. It has a necessary relationship with
man and his destiny, realities illumined by Christian faith. Moreover,

---

7. *Friends of God*, nos. 168, 172.

to see public life as totally separate from faith—or, in broader terms, separate from religion and God—leaves out a fundamental dimension of the human person and diminishes his or her dignity. It also belittles political activity. If civil society is not to be governed solely by utilitarian principles, with consequent harm to the human person, it will be necessary to set aside prejudices and reflect more deeply.

Fundamental to Christ's message regarding the right organization and functioning of political life is its affirmation of the primacy of the human being, created in God's image. Immersed in history and at the same time transcending it, a human person is a free and social being, called to work with other men and women in establishing relationships of service and mutual assistance and, more profoundly, of friendship and love. Its strong emphasis on personal freedom and transcendence sets the Christian message apart from all totalitarianisms systems, which submerge the individual in the collectivity. And because each person is called to communion and communication, it rules out any form of radical individualism, a vision of society as merely an aggregate of individuals, where the idea of the common good is replaced by the clash and balancing of private interests.

Jesus insisted that his kingdom is not of this world. He did not come to found an empire or to establish a movement or political party made up of his disciples. Jesus calls us to interior conversion, to faith, to an encounter with God the Father. Thus he initiates the family of God's children, the Church, whose mission is not to organize life in society, but to make Christ himself present in history, announcing his message and communicating his life, while respecting each person. And, as a liturgical hymn for the feast of the Epiphany points out, *Non eripit mortalia, qui regna dat coelestia,*—"He who instituted the Kingdom of Heaven, did not destroy temporal kingdoms."

This central event of history—the Incarnation of the Son of God—supplies light to see ourselves and society in a new way. For a true disciple of Jesus Christ, other people are never mere statistical data for doing business or winning an election, and still less are they regarded as rivals, enemies, or competitors. They are our brothers and sisters, because we are all children of our Father God.

While the Gospel message sheds light on fundamental political questions, it does not offer technical solutions to temporal problems. Christians receive from their faith inspiration and stimulus but no specific formulas for application to political or social questions. In these areas, everyone has the duty of making informed decisions about how he or she will act, without adulterating the content of the faith. As St. Josemaría said, a clear-thinking man will never describe himself as "stepping down from the temple into the world to represent the Church, or that his solutions are 'the Catholic solutions' to problems."[8]

Human dignity requires political and juridical structures that permit the free and effective participation of all citizens without discrimination. The authority of those who govern is grounded in the *legitimacy* of the procedures through which they have been designated to govern and in their effective service for the good of society and individuals.

Like any other citizen, a Christian is obliged to obey the laws, except in those cases—ordinarily, exceptional—when conscience requires opposing, even at times by civil disobedience, a law he considers unjust. In such a case, one should calmly accept the consequences of opposition to an unjust law, certain that one is acting in accord with God's will and for the good of one's fellow citizens. Mere passive compliance with law does not suffice. Everyone should participate actively, aware of his or her personal responsibility as a protagonist in the life of society. The *Catechism of the Catholic Church* calls this obligation of participation "inherent in the dignity of the human person."[9]

There are many forms of public activity in accord with the historical, social, and political circumstances of particular countries: civic associations, family and neighborhood organizations, labor unions,

---

8. *Conversations,* nos. 116–117.
9. *Catechism of the Catholic Church,* no. 1913.

business or craft associations, professional groups, etc. Important, too, are the media of communication—decisive in social life and contemporary politics—which provide public opinion with a means of expression while also contributing to its formation. And it goes without saying that Christians should exercise their right to vote in elections and referenda.

Many Christians have the gifts needed for political roles in the strict sense of the word: that is, direct participation in legislative or governmental institutions. Today, political activity typically means being involved in political parties and elections. Christians should frequently enter into this process in a spirit of cooperation and dialogue, always ready to learn from others. But always they should act in accord with their faith. In an extreme case, this can mean having to relinquish a political position, rather than cooperate with something scandalous because it is radically opposed to Christian doctrinal or moral convictions.

Recent history testifies that ideologies that ignore or deny man's openness to God undermine human dignity and can lead to violence. History testifies, too, to sacrifice and decisive action—sometimes heroic to the point of martyrdom—of believers who have taken their political role seriously. Christians render society a crucial service by being faithful to their beliefs.

The Gift of Joy

The prophets announced that the coming of the Messiah would bring happiness and joy. And when the fullness of time arrived, the first response to Jesus recorded in the Gospel was John the Baptist's joyful reaction, still in his mother's womb, when his mother Elizabeth was visited by Mary. "For behold, when the voice of your greeting came to my ears, the babe in my womb leaped for joy."[1] Even before his birth, Jesus' presence sowed joy.

So, too, the night of the Nativity witnessed an outpouring of joy. "Behold," proclaimed the angel, "I bring you good news of a great joy which will come to all the people; for to you is born this day in the city of David a Savior, who is Christ the Lord."[2] God's promises were fulfilled. The yearnings of the chosen people, and of all mankind, were abundantly answered.

When our liberation from sin through Christ's redemptive death was finally accomplished, and the gates of heaven opened with his resurrection, the Holy Spirit spread divine joy throughout the whole

---

1. Lk 1:44.
2. Lk 2:10–11.

world, starting on the day of Pentecost. The early Christian community worshipped with "glad and generous hearts."[3] "Great joy" took hold among the Samaritans when the Gospel was proclaimed to them. The Ethiopian who encountered the deacon Philip and received Baptism from his hands experienced great happiness. So did the jailer guarding St. Paul who, after the apostle's miraculous escape, was baptized along with his whole family.[4]

Joy, a Christian Gift

The proclamation of the Gospel is always accompanied by rejoicing. The Acts of the Apostles, and the New Testament as a whole, reveal how—when accepted into one's life with faith—the announcement of divine love, made visible through the Incarnation, produces great joy: deep and substantial joy, firmly rooted in the soul, that passing events cannot extinguish. Thus apostles, after their interrogation in the Sanhedrin, departed "rejoicing that they were counted worthy to suffer dishonor for the name."[5] St. Paul, as his second letter to the Corinthians records, found abundant joy amid great tribulation.

Suffering, whether physical or moral, can never steal joy and peace from the heart of a Christian closely united to our Lord. Joy will always be a clear mark of Christian life, for it is one of the fruits brought about by the presence of the Holy Spirit in our souls. No one is as happy as a true Christian, Paul said. Paul Claudel, affirmed that *only* a Christian has true joy, since faith never deceives.

"Renew your holy joy, for opposite the man who is decomposing without Christ, there is another who has risen with him."[6] These words of St. Josemaría, which alludes to the raising of Lazarus, indicate that, without a knowledge of the love of God revealed in Christ, people lose their direction in life; satisfaction comes to lie in perishable success or

3. Acts 2:46.
4. Cf. Acts 8:8, 38–39; 16:34.
5. Acts 5:41.
6. *The Forge*, no. 476.

pleasure; joy is unstable, sometimes even feigned. In contrast, one who grounds his life upon Christ and his Resurrection and his grace experiences every situation with the joy and peace that come from knowing God's fatherly love.

But the point in *The Forge* cited above can also be given another reading. St. Paul urges: "Put off your old nature which belongs to your former manner of life and is corrupt through deceitful lusts, and be renewed in the spirit of your minds, and put on the new nature, created after the likeness of God in true righteousness and holiness."[7] The man who is disintegrating is the "old man," the man centered on himself who lives in each of us. The man who is flourishing, the new man, is born in Baptism, and has begun to live with faith and love.

Christian joy is far removed from false contentment or the deceitful, momentary satisfaction of sin. It does not depend on "the happiness of a healthy animal,"[8] or the ups and downs of feelings, or the caprices of fortune. It is intimate and enduring, a result of Christian maturity, the response of the new man "created after the likeness of God in true righteousness and holiness."

Following Aristotle, St. Thomas Aquinas defines pleasure as enjoyment a creature experiences in attaining a good for which it has been made. Going further, he distinguishes between pleasure and joy or happiness, reserving the latter two terms for rational beings and signifying a good that reason perceives and approves.[9]

These considerations apply to human emotions viewed as spontaneous, instinctive powers. Pleasure or joy, seen this way, is more of an experience, a happening, than a virtuous act. St. Thomas elevates this perspective by considering these matters in relation to Christian life, specifically in light of the theological virtues and especially charity. What is the relationship between charity and joy? Is joy properly a virtue? Thomas's reply is that Christian joy is a true virtue because it

---

7. Eph 4:22, 24.
8. *The Way*, no. 659.
9. Cf. *Summa Theologica*, I–II, q. 31, a. 3.

involves a "certain act and effect of charity," that is, of the love for God that he infuses into us through the sending of the Holy Spirit.[10]

Christian's joy is not something external or merely a matter of feelings; it stems from faith and charity. We do not see God, but by faith we know the infinity of his love. From this knowledge, joy blossoms forth—if we truly believe, if our faith expresses itself in prayer. Faith, through the action of the Holy Spirit, leads us to recognize God's loving hand in each and every circumstance of life—even those painful and hard to understand—and to respond to God's love with our own love. Christian joy presupposes the liberation from uncertainty and sin that the Redemption brings about. Nourished by firmness in faith, it is expressed in a strong sense of divine filiation, which leads to a life lived in intimacy and harmony with God.

Sowers of Peace and Joy

A Christian spreads God's joy to others. St. Josemaría Escrivá liked to speak of Christians as *sowers of peace and joy*. "This is what the first Christians were," he wrote, "and this is what we have to be: sowers of peace and joy, the peace and joy that Jesus has brought to us."[11]

The use here of the word "sowers" implies that although we can speak about joy, joy above all spreads spontaneously through the example of our lives. That is how deep-lying attitudes are transmitted. If we are to sow peace and joy, they must first reign in our own hearts.

"Rejoice in the Lord always; again I say, rejoice."[12] Nothing and no one can destroy the peace of soul of someone who trusts fully in the Lord. St. Josemaría said: "If things go well, let us rejoice, blessing God who makes them prosper. And if they go badly? Let us rejoice, blessing God who allows us to share in the sweetness of his Cross."[13]

---

10. Cf. *Summa Theologica*, II–II, q. 28, a. 4.
11. *Christ Is Passing By*, no. 30.
12. Phil 4:4.
13. *The Way*, no. 658.

Not even the experience of one's own spiritual weakness can take away the joy of a child of God. Weaknesses should not lead to discouragement but to sorrow that, joined to trust in divine mercy, gives rise to contrition and impels one to return to the path with renewed vigor. "Be filled with wonder at God's goodness, for Christ wants to live in you. Be filled with wonder too when you are aware of all the weight of your poor flesh, of your wretched flesh, and all the vileness of the poor clay you are made of.—Yes, but then remember too that call from God: Jesus Christ, who is God and Man, understands me and looks after me, for he is my Brother and my Friend."[14]

Living in Christ and, in Christ, for God moves us to live in close union with our neighbor; it opens our hearts to such an extent that we can say with St. Thérèse of Lisieux: "Since I started never to seek myself, I have led the happiest life one could imagine." St. Josemaría said: "To give oneself sincerely to others is so effective that God rewards it with a humility filled with cheerfulness."[15]

But faith and love nevertheless can provoke a certain sadness in the Christian soul in response to the spectacle of evil and sin. Offenses against God hurt us deeply. Seeing how many failed to recognize Jesus as the Messiah, St. Paul wrote: "I have great sorrow and unceasing anguish in my heart."[16] But this holy sadness does not weigh down or paralyze the soul; it gives rise to trusting, insistent petition to God, in whose merciful and fatherly hands one places the concerns of one's heart.

In the end, there is only one true enemy of joy: sin, one's own sins and especially sins against faith that, by destroying love and trust in God, leave man in isolation.

Men or women of faith, their hearts on fire with love for God, may experience sickness and fatigue, hardship and anxiety. These things

14. *The Forge*, no. 182.
15. Ibid., no. 591.
16. Rom 9:2.

belong to the human condition. But such people lean constantly on God's strength and, with God's help, find joy amid the setbacks.

On the night of Holy Thursday, after urging the apostles to remain united to him as branches to the vine, Jesus said: "These things I have spoken to you, that my joy may be in you, and that your joy may be full."[17] He wants us to taste to the full his intimate joy, which will be fully realized on the day when—having traveled our path on earth with faith, hope, and charity—we hear the Master exclaim: "Well done, good and faithful servant; you have been faithful over a little, I will set you over much; enter into the joy of your master."[18] That immense happiness is too great for us to fathom now. But already we can begin to share in it if our faith is strong.

The Litany of Loreto salutes our Lady as "Cause of our joy." This title belongs to Mary for many reasons: because Jesus, our hope and our love, came to earth through her; because in contemplating her, we understand more fully the greatness and delicacy of God's love; because she herself, as Mother of God and our Mother, cares for each of us. Now and always let us invoke blessed Mary and her powerful intercession.

17. Jn 15:11.
18. Mt 25:23.